THE JOHN MUIR TRAIL

ABOUT THE AUTHOR

Alan Castle has trekked in over 25 countries within Europe, Asia, North and South America, Africa and Australasia, and for over 15 years has led organised walking holidays in several European countries. His longest solo walks include a Grand Traverse of the European Alps between Nice and Vienna (1510 miles), the Pilgrim's Trail from Le Puy to Santiago de Compostela (960 miles) and a coast-to-coast across the French Pyrenees (540 miles).

Alan has written more than a dozen walking guidebooks, several on long-distance mountain routes in France. He is a member of the British Outdoor Writers' Guild, and former national secretary and long-distance path information officer of the Long-Distance Walkers' Association. He now lives at the foot of the Moffat Hills in Scotland.

Other guidebooks by the author

The Grand Traverse of the Massif Central
The Robert Louis Stevenson Trail – Cévennes, France
The Southern Upland Way
Tour of the Queyras – French and Italian Alps
Walking in Bedfordshire
The River Rhine Trail
Walks in Volcano Country – Auvergne and Velay, France

In addition Alan wrote the first editions of Cicerone's guides to the GR20 through Corsica and to the GR10 through the French Pyrenees.

THE JOHN MUIR TRAIL

by
Alan Castle

2 POLICE SQUARE, MILNTHORPE, CUMBRIA LA7 7PY
www.cicerone.co.uk

© Alan Castle 2004. Reprinted with updates, 2006 and 2010
ISBN 10: 1 85284 396 9
ISBN 13: 978 1 85284 396 0

A catalogue record for this book is available from the British Library.
Photographs by the author, except for those on pages 91–95 by Charles Aitchison.

Printed by KHL Printing, Singapore

Dedication

This book is dedicated to my fellow hikers along the John Muir Trail, the other members of the Anglo-Scottish JMT Expedition 2001, without whom I could never have walked the Trail, and hence would never have written this guidebook: Charles Aitchison, Stewart Logan, Kim Mason, David Tattersfield and Andrew Wilkins.

Acknowledgements

I am particularly indebted to Charles Aitchison, retired Lakeland GP and expert naturalist, for contributing the section on the Natural World in the Introduction. I am grateful, as always, to my wife, Beryl Castle, for all her advice, support and encouragement during the planning and writing of this guidebook.

I would like to thank all those who have written or emailed since the publication of this guide offering useful additional information. This has been invaluable in updating the guide for its 2010 reprint. In particular I wish to thank Sue Allonby, Robert Francisco, Kevin Freer, Linda Jeffers, Susan Lien, Tim Mason, Cameron McNeish, Craig Miller, Jeff Parr and Ronald Turnbull.

Warning

Front cover: Hiker on the JMT near Muir Trail Ranch (Day 11)

CONTENTS

The Natural World

TRAIL GUIDE 103

Yosemite Valley

APPENDICES

The tendency nowadays to wander in wildernesses is delightful to see. Thousands of tired, nerve-shaken, over-civilized people are beginning to find out that going to the mountains is going home; that wildness is a necessity; and that mountain parks and reservations are useful not only as fountains of timber and irrigating rivers, but as fountains of life.

John Muir, *Our National Parks* (1901)

Climb the mountains and get their good tidings. Nature's peace will flow into you as sunshine flows into trees. The winds will blow their own freshness into you, and the storms their energy, while cares will drop off like autumn leaves.

John Muir (1838–1914)

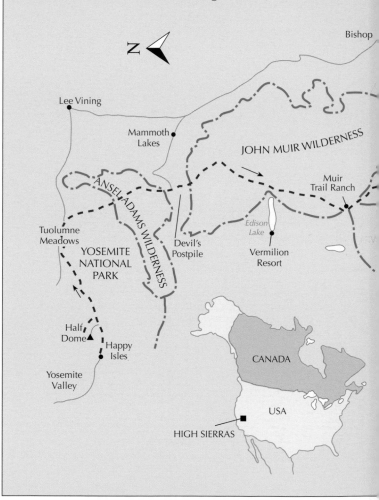

The John Muir Trail in the High Sierras of California

N

Bishop

Lee Vining

Mammoth Lakes

JOHN MUIR WILDERNESS

Muir Trail Ranch

ANSEL ADAMS WILDERNESS

Tuolumne Meadows

YOSEMITE NATIONAL PARK

Devil's Postpile

Edison Lake

Vermilion Resort

Half Dome

Happy Isles

Yosemite Valley

CANADA

USA

HIGH SIERRAS

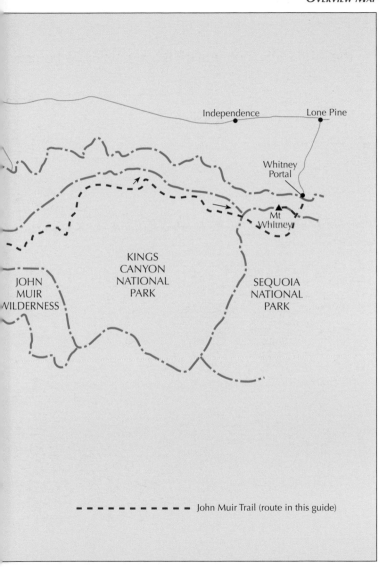

John Muir Trail (route in this guide)

Map Key

– – – – – ·	John Muir Trail
– – – – – ·	John Muir Trail (route in this guide)
⟶	Route direction
··············	Side trails
—·—·—·—	National Park/Wilderness Area boundary
∼∼∼	River/stream
≈∼∼	Road
R	Ranger station
×	Day stage camp area
▲	Peak
⊗	Official campsite
⬭	Lake/tarn

TRAIL SUMMARY TABLE

Day	Stage	Distance (miles)	Ascent (ft)	Descent (ft)
1	Yosemite Valley (Happy Isles) to Half Dome Trail Junction/Sunrise Creek and the Ascent of Half Dome	12.3	5000	1850
2	Half Dome Trail Junction/Sunrise Creek to Sunrise High Sierra Camp	7.6	2600	400
3	Sunrise High Sierra Camp, via Cathedral Pass to Tuolumne Meadows	11.4	400	1200
Rest	Tuolumne Meadows	–	–	–
4	Tuolumne Meadows to Upper Lyell Canyon	9.5	1200	100
5	Upper Lyell Canyon via Donohue Pass and Island Pass to Thousand Island Lake	9.7	2200	1950
6	Thousand Island Lake to the Devil's Postpile	16.2	1800	4100
7	The Devil's Postpile to Deer Creek	9.0	1700	150
8	Deer Creek to Tully Hole/Cascade Valley Junction	12.3	2050	2050
9	Tully Hole/Cascade Valley Junction via Silver Pass to Edison Lake	11.8	1850	3150
Rest	Vermilion Resort	–	–	–
10	Edison Lake to Rosemarie Meadow	12.3	3350	1050
11	Rosemarie Meadow via Selden Pass to the Muir Trail Ranch	9.5	1050	3350
12	Muir Trail Ranch to McClure Meadow	10.6	2200	200
13	McClure Meadow via Muir Pass to unnamed lake north-east of Helen Lake	12.2	2450	1300
14	Unnamed lake north-east of Helen Lake to Deer Meadow	11.3	1000	2900
15	Deer Meadow via Mather Pass to Kings River	12.0	3300	2000
16	Kings river via Pinchot Pass to Woods Creek	11.6	2050	3700
17	Woods Creek via Glen Pass to Vidette Meadow	13.2	3650	2600
18	Vidette Meadow via Forester Pass to Tyndall Creek	12.0	3800	2500
19	Tyndall Creek to Guitar Lake	12.1	1800	1200
20	Guitar Lake via Mount Whitney and Trail Crest to Trail Camp and the Ascent of Mount Whitney	10.0	3200	2600
21	Trail Camp to Whitney Portal	6.8	50	3700
Totals		**233.4**	**46,700**	**42,050**

Hiker on the steep descent from Forester Pass (Day 18)

INTRODUCTION

BACKGROUND

The John Muir Trail (JMT) is one of the world's greatest treks and is North America's best-known mid-distance walking trail. It runs for 216 miles through the high Sierra Nevada mountains of California, from Yosemite Valley in the north to the summit of Mount Whitney (14,496ft) above Lone Pine in the south, and takes about three weeks to complete.

The route is largely a wilderness experience, and this intensifies as one progresses along the Trail from the relative civilisation between Yosemite and Tuolumne, where there are many day-trippers and other walkers, to the huge wilderness areas further south, particularly after the Muir Trail Ranch. Tourists are once again encountered, in the form of day walkers on Mount Whitney, during the very last stages of the Trail.

However, although the JMT passes through areas of genuine wilderness, the Trail by its very nature confines backpackers to a narrow corridor through that wilderness. The Trail was man made and is maintained by rangers, and along its length there are Ranger Stations where officials are found during the summer season. You will undoubtedly pass many other hikers during your sojourn along the JMT, and will rarely be more than a

The Edison Queen approaching Mono Creek ferry pick-up point (Day 9)

mile or two from other human beings. Only by leaving the man-made trails would one truly be entering the huge wilderness that is the Californian High Sierras.

While the John Muir Trail passes through high mountain country where spectacular peaks and high passes abound, the JMT itself is a relatively easy trail to walk. Gradients are rarely very steep, as the trail was expertly engineered and was originally intended for pack animals, mules and horses. So although the JMT often goes over high passes, the routes over them are nearly always well graded. You may, however, marvel that horses were expected to traverse such narrow and dramatic trails as those over the Forester and Glen passes; both an experienced rider and horse would be necessary!

There is little in the way of exposure along the entire length of the JMT, no scrambling is involved and no particular head for heights is required. The only exception is perhaps on the descent from the Forester Pass, but most mountain walkers would hardly give even this a second thought. The ascent of Half Dome, which is not part of the JMT, is a rather different matter. The climb to the top of the mountain is over very steep and polished granite, but the route is well protected and those with some scrambling ability in the mountains should again have no worries. Navigation along the Trail is relatively straightforward, and users of this guidebook who also carry

the recommended maps for the JMT should experience few route-finding problems. The Trail is well way-marked on the ground. Note that the above analysis, of course, applies only to good summer conditions; snowed- and iced-up passes and rivers in spate would be altogether far more difficult and dangerous.

The Route

While the official Trail runs for 216 miles, the fact that it terminates on the top of Mount Whitney, the highest point in the 48 contiguous States of the US, means that the route is, in reality, somewhat longer, as walkers must descend and return to civilisation. There is a good continuing trail from Mount Whitney down to the roadhead at Whitney Portal to the east, and this is the one usually used to finish the JMT.

The dramatic peak of Half Dome lies a little off the route of the JMT at the northern end of the trail in Yosemite National Park, and few adventurous walkers would want to pass by without making a detour to climb this sensational mountain.

With these two extensions to the JMT the total distance of the trek amounts to some 233 miles, with a total cumulative ascent of about 46,700ft (14,234m), over 1½ times the height of Everest. By walking from north to south the total descent is only around 42,000ft (12,800m), as Yosemite Valley lies at a much lower altitude than Whitney Portal.

Much of the JMT is coincident with the ultra-long-distance Pacific Crest Trail (PCT) that crosses the western US north to south between the Canadian and Mexican borders.

The first section of the JMT heads eastwards through Yosemite, passing Vernal and Nevada waterfalls and to the south of Half Dome to Sunrise High Sierra Camp and then north-eastwards over the Cathedral Range to reach a second roadhead at Tuolumne Meadows. A café/snack bar, store and post office here are useful to JMT walkers before the long journey south to Whitney begins.

From Tuolumne a long ascent up the wide and beautiful Lyell Valley leads to the first high pass of the JMT, the 11,056ft Donohue Pass, where the Trail leaves Yosemite National Park to enter the Ansel Adams Wilderness Area in Inyo National Forest. The route then heads south-eastwards across a landscape dotted with a multitude of mountain lakes and tarns – Thousand Island Lake, Emerald Lake, Garnet Lake and Shadow Lake – all beneath the dominating and shapely summits of Mount Ritter and Banner Peak.

A long descent southwards through woodland leads to the Devil's Postpile National Monument, massive columnar blocks of basalt resembling those found at the Giant's Causeway in Ireland. Nearby the wilderness walker can enjoy both the hot tubs at the thermal springs and Reds Meadow Resort, which offers the hungry hiker a restaurant/café and a store selling basic foodstuffs.

The trail now climbs through trees that were badly burned in a forest fire in the early 1990s

Half Dome from Yosemite Valley (Day 1)

15

Hikers on the JMT climbing towards the Pinchot Pass (Day 16)

to pass into the huge John Muir Wilderness to reach Deer Creek, before following a trail of volcanic dust along a ridge heading south-eastwards high above Cascade Valley. Duck Lake is by-passed, but the undulating JMT passes Purple Lake and Lake Virginia before dropping steeply down to Tully Hole. Lakes named after the Native American culture (Squaw Lake, Chief Lake, Papoose Lake) are passed on the ascent to the Trail's second major pass, Silver Pass at 10,900ft. A long descent southwards follows, past Silver Pass Lake and Pocket Meadow to reach Quail Meadows, a short distance east of Edison Lake. Most JMT walkers will then want to take the ferry boat trip across this lake to spend a day or two

relaxing at Vermilion Resort, where there is always a special welcome awaiting JMT and PCT Thru-Hikers.

After crossing Mono Creek the Trail rises steeply to attain Bear Ridge, which eventually drops to Bear Creek. This mountain stream is followed to Upper Bear Creek Meadows and then up to Rosemarie Meadows, past Marie Lake and over the Seldon Pass, which lies at the same altitude as its northern neighbour, at 10,900ft. The JMT descends past Heart Lake and Sallie Keyes Lake to reach Muir Trail Ranch, the last place en route where food caches may be collected.

From here on there is no compromise as the Trail enters a huge wilderness area between Muir Trail Ranch and the end of the Trail, climbing virtually every day over increasingly higher mountain passes. The Trail heads south-eastwards along the South Fork of the San Joaquin river to enter Kings Canyon National Park at Piute Creek. The San Joaquin river is left behind at Goddard Canyon as the JMT turns at first eastwards to head up Evolution Valley. Three lush meadows are passed on the way to Evolution Lake, from where a high alpine world is entered as the Trail passes Sapphire, Wanda (named after Muir's daughter) and McDermand Lakes to climb to the pass named after the great man himself. Muir Pass, at 11,955ft, is the only col on the JMT to boast a man-made building, a stone shelter hut.

The descent on the far side of the pass leads past Helen Lake (named after Muir's other daughter) before dropping down Le Conte Canyon, passing Big Pete and Little Pete Meadows. After Grouse Meadows the Trail turns eastwards to ascend alongside Palisade Creek to reach Deer Meadow. A sensational path, steep and terraced, then leads upwards to the Palisade Lakes, above which towers Mather Pass (12,100ft), the first pass above 12,000ft encountered on the Trail. The broad, desert-like Upper Basin leads down to the Kings river, after which another climb takes the hiker over the 12,130ft Pinchot Pass and so down to Woods Creek, which is spanned by a most impressive suspension footbridge.

The JMT follows the South Fork of Woods Creek, passing Dollar,

Arrowhead and Rae Lakes before climbing to 11,978ft at Glen Pass. A descent follows to Bubbs Creek, the valley of which is then ascended into more and more rocky terrain beneath the dramatic Junction Peak. Forester Pass (13,180ft), the first time that the Trail climbs to over 13,000ft, is attained at the Kings Kern Divide, allowing entry into the Mount Whitney area of the High Sierras.

The JMT bids farewell to its big brother travel companion, the Pacific Crest Trail, a little before Crabtree Meadow. The appropriately shaped Guitar Lake lies below and to the west of the Whitney massif, and from here a zig-zagging climb leads to Trail Junction, where backpacks can be thankfully abandoned for a time while Mount Whitney (14,496ft) itself is climbed. The last pass of the journey is Trail Crest (13,600ft), which is easily attained before the seemingly never-ending descent leads out of the wilderness down to Whitney Portal.

Walking a Wilderness Trail

For British backpackers and long-distance path walkers, the major difference between the JMT and long-distance routes in Britain and western Europe is the large expanses of wilderness through which the JMT passes where there is no permanent human habitation and no basic facilities. The only possible form of accommodation is a backpacking tent, and the only food available is that carried in by walkers themselves. There are no cafés, restaurants, mountain huts or B&Bs – nothing whatsoever.

In Britain and much of Europe, should weather conditions take turn for the worse, or if you fancy a bit of luxury, it is nearly always possible to opt for a night in a hotel or have a meal in a restaurant. With one or two exceptions, you will generally not have such an option while on the JMT.

Again, there is little need in most parts of western Europe for backpackers to carry more than one or two day's worth of food, because villages and towns with shops and restaurants are encountered fairly regularly. Nowhere would you be compelled to carry up to ten day's worth of food, as on the southern section of the JMT. Careful planning is required to ensure that you have sufficient food while walking the Trail, and you must be completely self-reliant.

Walkers should also be aware that the national parks and official wilderness areas of the US are subject to a range of regulations designed to protect ecologically sensitive areas (see 'Low impact trekking and national park/wilderness regulations', in 'Walking the Trail', below).

While the JMT should present no real difficulties for the seasoned hill and long-distance walker, it is recommended that those undertaking it have previously walked at least one continuous route of more than 150 miles in length, preferably in the Scottish Highlands, Alps or Pyrenees, before attempting the JMT. Some experience at a reasonably high altitude would be an advantage.

If you are concerned that all the planning and physical effort required to walk the John Muir Trail is a little beyond you, then do consider the achievements of Al (Albert) Ansorge from Illinois, who in 2001, when over 80 years old, completed his tenth walk along the entire John Muir Trail. Al made his first JMT trek in 1981 when a mere youngster in his sixties. He reckons that the JMT is the best hike in the world, and this author could not disagree with that opinion.

JOHN MUIR

John Muir (1838–1914) is a household name in the US. This somewhat eccentric man – naturalist, conservationist, sage, explorer, mountaineer, inventor, writer and founding father of the national park movement – is alas largely unknown, except to outdoor enthusiasts, in the land where he was born and grew up, Scotland. It is hoped that this guidebook will in some small way help to make the name of John Muir, together with his philosophy, principles of conservation and respect for the wild places of this planet, better known to a wider audience.

John Muir was born on April 21st 1838 in Dunbar on the east coast of Scotland, in Lothian. He was the son of a strict Calvinist and tyrannical disciplinarian who worked his sons harshly. In 1849 the family decided to emigrate to the New World, and so at the age of eleven John left his homeland to make a new life in the United States of America. The family settled on Hickory Hill Farm, near Portage in Wisconsin. In his free time John learnt to wander the open, unfenced country of the neighbourhood, and at this early age developed the love of the outdoors that was to remain with him all his life. He was largely self-taught during these formative years, hiding his reading from his father, who disapproved of book learning. John discovered that he had a gift for invention as well as for geology and botany, and with these talents entered the University of Wisconsin in 1860.

After three years of higher education Muir did various odd jobs, living for a while in Canada to escape the Civil War in the States, but it wasn't until an accident that nearly blinded

him in 1867 that he determined to wander widely. His first long trek was 1000 miles from Indianapolis to the Gulf of Mexico. He next sailed to Cuba with the intention of travelling down to South America, but instead changed his plans to head north for San Francisco where he landed in March 1868.

It was a decision that was to change the whole direction of his life. At the age of 30 he entered Yosemite for the first time and was awe-struck by what he saw. 'I only took a walk in the Yosemite,' he later said, 'but stayed for six years'. California, and particularly Yosemite and the Sierra Nevada, would become his home, both physically and spiritually. To Muir the Sierra Nevada was 'the Range of Light...the most divinely beautiful of all the mountain chains I have ever seen.'

Octogenarian Al Ansorge (seated far left) in Vermilion Valley Resort dining room during his tenth trek along the JMT

John Muir had considerable mountaineering talents, being attributed with the first ascent of Mount Ritter and with one of the early winter ascents of Half-Dome. But it is for becoming the first conservationist that he is really remembered. Muir was one of the first people to study the science of ecology and to witness at first hand, from his pine cabin home in Yosemite, the damaging effects of the hand of man. He developed a theory of glaciation to explain the formation of Yosemite Valley, and in 1874 started his career as a successful and influential writer. At the age of 42 in 1880 Muir married Louise Strentzel and moved to Martinez, California (now a John Muir National Historic Site), where he ran a fruit farm and brought up his family of two daughters, Helen and Wanda. JMT walkers will pass two mountain lakes that were named after these daughters, either side of the Muir Pass (Day 13). He still managed to travel widely, visiting Alaska, South America, Africa, Australia and elsewhere. He returned to Scotland on only one occasion, to the Highlands, Dunbar, Edinburgh and Dumfries, in 1893.

Through his writings and eccentric lifestyle Muir became widely known throughout the United States. He was an influential figure who received the rich and famous to his simple Californian home, including the poet and essayist Ralph Emerson, the author and naturalist H.D. Thoreau and the eminent geologist Joseph Le Conte (see Le Conte Canyon, Day14 of the JMT). Muir was a confidant of congressmen, presidents and other influential people, and in this way was able to persuade the most

One of the numerous mountain tarns below Silver Pass (Day 9)

powerful men in the country of the urgent need to protect the wilderness areas of western America from commercial exploitation. He pushed for the establishment of Yosemite as the first national park in 1890. In 1903 Muir encouraged President Roosevelt to spend several nights camping out in Yosemite with him, during which time they agreed on a programme of conservation for the area.

Muir was also instrumental in the fight to set up Sequoia, Grand Canyon and other national parks for reasons of conservation and access, and is today dubbed the founding father of America's national park system. The debate over national parks was really a debate about exploitation versus conservation. In a land where capitalism and the work ethic reign supreme it is perhaps surprising that Muir's views won the day and that the national parks in America were established to protect and conserve the great wildernesses so early on in the country's history.

John Muir was undoubtedly America's most famous and influential naturalist and conservationist, but he was also a popular writer whose somewhat romantic style and unbounded love of nature often won over the hearts even of those with little interest in nature and the environment. His eight wilderness books, a lifetime's work, are classics of the genre: *The Story of my Boyhood and Youth, A Thousand Mile Walk to the Gulf, My First Summer in the Sierra, The Mountains of California, Our National Parks, The Yosemite, Travels in Alaska* and *Steep Trails*. They were republished in Britain by Diadem in one volume in 1992 (see Appendix 7 – Bibliography). In all he wrote over 300 articles and 10 major books.

Sadly Muir lost his last fight, a long, drawn-out campaign to save the Hetch Hetchy Valley in Yosemite from being flooded. This failure dispirited him and soon after, on Christmas Eve 1914, he died of pneumonia.

His lasting memorials are the world's national park networks established by those inspired by his vision. His views are perhaps even more relevant today because of the many threats that the modern world poses for the wild places of this fragile planet. In essence Muir's naturalist philosophy was a simple one, believing that man truly belonged to nature. 'I only went out for a walk,' he wrote, 'and finally decided to stay out till sundown, for going out, I found, was really going in.'

In Memory of John Muir

In Britain the memory of John Muir, the principles by which he lived and his life's work in saving and conserving wild areas of the world are embodied in the John Muir Trust, a charity founded in 1983. The aims of the trust are simple: to save and conserve wild places. At the time of writing the it owns and manages seven outstanding wild areas, totalling over 20,000 hectares in the

On the JMT in Yosemite en route to Nevada Falls (Day 1)

Highlands and Islands of Scotland, including Britain's highest mountain, Ben Nevis. The trust is a membership organisation open to all who have an interest in wild places. A regular journal keeps members informed of activities and plans for the future. Further details of the trust can be found on their website at www.jmt.org (see Appendix 6).

Efforts have also been made during recent years to raise the profile of John Muir in his native Scotland. The John Muir Birthplace Trust was founded in September 1998 as a partnership project involving East Lothian Council, the John Muir Trust, Dunbar's John Muir Association and Dunbar Community Council. The aim of the trust is to secure the future of John Muir's birthplace in Dunbar

and an interpretative centre, focused on Muir's work, was opened there in 2003. It is now visited by thousands of tourists from all over the world, and provides projects for hundreds of local schoolchildren.

Also in memory of John Muir, East Lothian Council has completed a new long distance path in South-East Scotland, opened in September 2007. The John Muir Way (not Trail!) runs for 45 miles, from Cockburnspath (eastern end of the Southern Upland Way) via Dunbar to the edge of Edinburgh, part of the ultra-long North Sea Coastal Trail. The Way, of course, offers a very different experience to the Trail, but is nevertheless a fitting memorial on this side of the Atlantic, to the founding father of the world wide National Park movement.

PARKS ALONG THE JMT

The John Muir Trail passes through three of North America's finest and best-known national parks.

Yosemite is known the world over for its high, spectacular mountains and for some of the most stunning, high and technically difficult rock faces anywhere on earth. Few outdoor people will not know of Half Dome and El Capitan, the latter a huge rock monolith (the largest single granite rock on earth) towering above Yosemite Valley and very popular with the world's top climbers. Yosemite is a natural wonderland of high mountains, granite cliffs, waterfalls, alpine lakes, tarns and streams. Two of the world's ten highest waterfalls are found in the park, Upper Yosemite and Ribbon Falls.

Situated in the High Sierras of central California, Yosemite was one of America's first National Parks (Yellowstone was the first in 1872). It was in fact the first area of the States to be given special protection by an act of Congress in 1864, but was not officially designated a national park until 1st October 1890, due largely to the work and sterling efforts of Muir, President Theodore Roosevelt and other influential figures..

Almost 95% of the 750,000 acre park is unspoilt wilderness. Today it is one of America's most visited national parks, with over 4 million visitors annually. Most, however, visit only the visitor centre, shops, cafés, restaurants and other amenities of Yosemite Valley, whilst the more adventurous do a day-hike or two from Yosemite Valley or Tuolumne Meadows. For those with a head for heights the ascent of Half Dome is a very popular day-hike from Yosemite Valley. But only a tiny percentage of Yosemite's visitors venture deep into its wilderness. You are to be one of these most fortunate people who will cross the wilderness of Yosemite, experiencing this most awe-inspiring of mountain landscapes.

Today **Kings Canyon and Sequoia** national parks in the southern Sierra share a boundary and are administered as one park. However, they were set up by separate acts of Congress at different times, and a little of their history will help to make clear their importance. In the mid-18th century this land was seen as ripe for commercial exploitation and attracted timber barons who came to fell the mighty and ancient trees that grew here. But such enlightened and influential people as John Muir worked hard to obtain protection for this special wilderness area.

In 1890, very soon after the creation of Yosemite National Park, the second US national park was established, the relatively small Sequoia National Park, 50,000 acres of protected land. Just a week later a third but very tiny national park (2500 acres) was designated as the General Grant National Park (named after the

American general and 18th president of the US, who had died five years earlier in 1885). At the same time more land was added to Sequoia National Park, tripling its size. The continuing efforts of conservationists over the years led to further expansion of the two parks, until in 1940 General Grant National Park took in land around the South Fork Kings river and changed its name to Kings Canyon National Park. As late as 1965 Cedar Grove and Tehipite Valley were added to the park.

The combined Kings Canyon and Sequoia national parks amount to over 1300 square miles of mountain and forest wilderness. The elevation range is from as low as 1500ft in the low foothills of the west of the parks to the high mountains of the Great Western Divide and High Sierras in the east. The highest point in continental America (or the contiguous states), the 14,496ft-high Mount Whitney, lies on the border of Sequoia National Park.

By far the majority of the park lies within the Sequoia and Kings Canyon Wilderness Area; so, as in Yosemite, few of the 2 million annual visitors to the parks reach the heartland of this stunning area. The parks are famous for their Sequoias, the world's largest trees. The best examples are to be found in the north of the parks area, in the Giant Forest plateau. Here can be found the tallest of the Sequoias, the 275ft-high 'General Sherman', whose trunk has a ground-level circumference of 103ft and which weighs an estimated 1385 tons.

John Muir Wilderness

In honour and recognition of the life's work of America's best-known conservationist and father of the national parks a large tract of land in California has been designated the John Muir Wilderness.

Located in the Inyo and Sierra national forests, the 581,000-acre John Muir Wilderness is the largest wilderness area in California. Some of the most spectacular mountain scenery on earth is to be seen there, and it is perhaps not surprising that it is the most visited wilderness in the state of California. This unspoilt backcountry is characterised by mile after mile of high snow-capped mountain ranges, countless sparkling alpine lakes, tarns, waterfalls, rivers and streams flowing with crystal-clear pure waters, and vast stretches of native forest. This is all high country, with elevation ranging between 4000 and 14,000ft.

Both the John Muir Trail and the Pacific Crest Trail pass through this wilderness. The JMT first enters the John Muir Wilderness at Red Cones on Day 7 of the trek, leaving on Day 12 when Kings Canyon National Park is entered, soon after leaving Muir Trail Ranch. The very last stages of the hike, Days 20 and 21, from Trail Crest down to Whitney Portal, also cross the John Muir Wilderness.

View of the summit crags on Mount Whitney (Day 20)

Ansel Adams and the Ansel Adams Wilderness

The John Muir Trail passes through an area known as the Ansel Adams Wilderness (on Days 5, 6 and 7, from the Donohue Pass, where the Trail leaves the Yosemite National Park, to Red Cones south of Reds Meadow, where the JMT enters the John Muir Wilderness).

Ansel Adams (1902–1984) was one of America's foremost landscape photographers and conservationists. Born in San Francisco at the beginning of the 20th century, Ansel Adams rejected a conventional formal education, but showed an early interest in nature and the Californian wilderness after a boyhood trip with his family to Yosemite in 1916, just two years after John Muir's death.

Adams's early inclination was to become a pianist, but his interest in photography deepened, and by the late 1920s he was beginning to be recognised as a landscape photographer of outstanding talent. He is particularly well known for his photographs of the national parks of western US. He used his photographs to further his work on conservation, persuading politicians that the great wilderness areas of the US were worth protecting. He served on the board of the influential Sierra Club, founded by Muir in 1892, for nearly 40 years. Ansel Adams died at the age of 82 in April 1984.

His life's work in landscape photography and conservation has been honoured by the designation of part of the Californian High Sierra wilderness as the Ansel Adams Wilderness.

THE PACIFIC CREST TRAIL

The Pacific Crest Trail (PCT) is the father or perhaps the very big brother of the John Muir Trail. The US has three great ultra-long walking trails that stretch from north to south across this huge country. The Appalachian Trail in the east was the first to be established in 1937. It starts in the southern state of Georgia and heads north for 2100 miles to finish in Maine near the Canadian border. The newest, longest and hardest of the three is the Continental Divide Trail, which runs between Mexico and Canada along the watershed of the United States. But perhaps the most impressive in terms of the grandeur and diversity of its scenery is the Pacific Crest Trail, which also stretches from Mexico to Canada, but through the three western states of California, Oregon and Washington, a total distance of 2665 miles.

Although the PCT coincides with the JMT for much of the length of the latter, there are sections where the two long-distance paths go their own ways. In particular the JMT and PCT do not coincide at the northern end of the JMT (ie. between Yosemite Valley and Tuolumne Meadows) and at the southern terminus of the JMT (the PCT leaves the JMT a little before Crabtree Ranger Station and omits the traverse of Mount Whitney). In all about 175 miles of the JMT are coincident with the PCT.

The PCT is a trail of extremes, as it passes through six of the seven ecological zones of North America, from near sea level to over 13,000ft in altitude, from the ferociously hot deserts of southern California to the High Sierra mountains, from the temperate rain forests of the Pacific North-West to the volcanic peaks and glaciers of the Cascade Mountains. The highlights include the Mojave Desert; the Sierra Nevada including Yosemite, Kings Canyon and Sequoia national parks; Marble Mountain and the Russian Wilderness in Northern California; the volcanoes of the Cascades, including Mount Shasta and Mount Hood; Crater

Pacific Crest/John Muir Trail signpost just outside Tuolumne Meadows (Day 4)

Lake; Columbia River Gorge; Mount Rainier; and the Northern Cascades.

Every year around 300 or more of the world's best long-distance backpackers gather at the end of April for the now traditional send-off party near the Mexican border, and the following day take their first steps northwards on a truly marathon hike through the US to Canada. Many of these 'Thru-Hikers' fail to complete the PCT in one season, but the determined few make it to Canada by early October.

Nearly all PCT Thru-Hikers head north because the logistics of walking north to south in one season are unfeasible. Most head through the High Sierra country through which the JMT passes during the month of June, so they have to contend with much more snow than the summertime JMT walker, and river crossings can be extremely hazardous as the many streams are swollen by melting snows high up in the mountains.

The chances of a southbound JMT hiker during the summertime encountering a northbound PCT Thru-Hiker are therefore pretty slight. However, for every Thru-Hiker there are many hundreds of other backpackers who walk sections of the PCT every year, and you are sure to see some of these. It is the cherished ambition of some American backpackers to complete the PCT over a number of seasons, and many do a week, fortnight or monthly stage every year. Most take half a lifetime or more to complete the Trail.

Many thousands more are content to return to the wilderness occasionally for short adventures of a few day's duration.

The Pacific Crest Trail Association (PCTA – see Appendix 6) is the best source of information for anyone contemplating an attempt of all or a section of the PCT, perhaps after their appetite has been whetted by first walking the JMT. But do remember that the JMT is only about 10% of the length of the PCT. After a few days on the JMT you will no doubt have great respect for PCT Thru-Hikers! The PCTA also provides good, reliable information on the JMT.

NOTES ON USING THE GUIDEBOOK

This next two sections of this Introduction, 'Planning Your Trip' and 'Walking the Trail', could be subtitled 'Before You Go', because they give all the information needed to plan and organise a hike along the JMT. There is greater emphasis on the preparation and planning stages of this walk than is usual in guidebooks to long-distance routes in Europe and the UK and/or routes where there are no sections in extensive areas of wilderness. This emphasis on pre-route planning is deliberate, and is imperative with an adventure such as the JMT; good preparation will result in a happy, stress-free trek, and provide you with one of the most incredible experiences of your life. Topics such as hiking in bear country, applying for wilderness trekking permits, the filtering of water and the danger of giardiasis, and the packaging and posting ahead of food packages for collection along the Trail, which may not be familiar to walkers from outside the US, are an essential part of hiking the JMT and are explained in detail.

The 'Route Guide' describes the route of the John Muir Trail. The Trail has been divided into 21 stages, each of a day's duration, although inevitably some stages are longer and/or harder than others. Each day stage has been designed to end at an area where there are good or at least reasonable camping possibilities (these are listed in Appendix 1), although other places where a camp could be set up are also indicated. The average reasonably fit and experienced backpacker should be able to cover this itinerary comfortably each day. Some may wish to travel further and faster, and certainly a very fit walker would have no trouble in doing so. But this is mountain country of really outstanding character and natural beauty, and to move fast through this landscape would in many respects be defeating the whole reason for being there. Savour this spectacular wilderness. A few hikers may wish to travel more slowly, but those who do so must carry more food supplies. This is not a problem on the first half of the Trail, but to take longer than the suggested time on the southern section of the JMT, from Muir Trail Ranch to Whitney Portal, would require carrying in excess of 10 days' worth of food, or else making very lengthy detours to restock supplies.

Cathedral Peak (Day 3)

What's in a Name?
It is interesting how different English words are used around the world for the basic task of putting one foot in front of the other. In Britain this activity is known as 'walking' or 'rambling'; in the Himalayas or in Patagonia and elsewhere it is 'trekking'; in New Zealand it is 'tramping' and in Australia 'bushwalking'. In the US people go 'hiking', which is now considered a very old-fashioned term in Britain. But for some inexplicable reason 'hiking' seems just right to describe the activity of walking through the American wilderness, and is used frequently in this book.

Each day stage opens with two tables. The first gives the total distance for the stage, the cumulative distance from the start of the Trail at Yosemite, the total ascent and descent for the stage, and the cumulative figures for ascent and descent from Yosemite. (The total ascents and descents for each stage are given to the nearest 50ft.) The length and severity of the stage can thus be gleaned at a glance. The second table gives a breakdown of the route, with heights above sea level of the various intermediary points and a breakdown of distances between these locations, allowing progress during the day to be easily assessed. Next, the map sheet number(s) required (from the recommended Harrison JMT Map-Pack; see 'Maps', below) for the stage is given for easy reference.

The route description opens with a summary intended to give an overview of the day, and could be read in camp the evening before to give a feel for the nature of the following day's trek. Finally a detailed route description is given, with the main features and places in **bold**, which is intended for use on the Trail.

Topographical height versus distance profiles are provided to enable the amount of ascent and descent along the Trail to be easily assessed, and sketch maps of the route allow the user to gain an overview of the trail for planning purposes. The sketch maps and guidebook are designed to be used in conjunction with the relevant Harrison Map-Pack. One should never venture out into wilderness areas, even on a waymarked trail, without an accurate and detailed map.

The book ends with a number of appendices which contain detailed and summarised information for both the planning stages and when out on the Trail.

The abbreviations JMT (John Muir Trail) and PCT (Pacific Crest Trail) are used. The term 'Trail', with a capital 'T', refers to the John Muir Trail, while 'trail' indicates a side-trail or path other than the JMT.

Distances are given in miles and yards, and heights in feet, as the US uses the imperial system. American maps are also in imperial units, unlike those of the UK and continental Europe. Generally, metric conversions have not been given in the text.

Most distances in miles that appear in the guidebook have been estimated from maps, but when a signpost/board is mentioned in the text the distances stated are those given on the signpost, as this should be an aid to locating your position on the Trail.

No attempt has been made to assign walking times to individual sections. Different people tackling the JMT will have different levels of fitness, and while some like to move fast in the mountains others prefer to progress at a much more leisurely pace. The data on distance and ascent/descent at the start of each day stage should allow the walker who knows his own strengths and weaknesses to estimate how long a particular section will take to cover. But remember that if you are part of a group the progress of the party will be determined by the speed of the slowest member.

Remember also that at the higher altitudes on the Trail, particularly in the southern half of the JMT, a walker's rate of ascent in the relatively thin air is likely to be slower than at lower elevations. Daytime temperature, which can often be high even at altitude, will also affect progress.

PLANNING YOUR TRIP

In countries such as the UK it is possible to walk the Pennine Way, for example, at a moment's notice: pack a tent and backpack, perhaps make a few phone calls to B&Bs, catch a train and then simply … go! It is not possible to walk the JMT in this manner. Only careful pre-trip planning will ensure a trouble-free walk along the JMT with sufficient food and the right equipment.

First, questions must be asked about the direction in which to hike the Trail and the right time of year to do so; whether to walk alone or with a group. Note also that, unlike the UK and most of Europe, permits are required to walk in wilderness areas of the United States (see 'Wilderness Permits', below), and they are strictly allocated to ensure the trails are not overused. A permit must be applied for several months in advance of the trip, preferably before a flight is booked to the States. Thought has also to be given to the means of getting from the airport of arrival to the trailhead and back to an airport at the end of the walk, not particularly a straightforward thing to achieve in public-transport-shy America.

There are few places along the Trail where meals can be bought, so food for the whole trip must be purchased and much of it packaged up and posted to a collection point further down the Trail. Water in the wilds of California is generally unsafe

Granite boulders on the summit of Half Dome (Day 1)

to drink and so it is vital to take some means of making it safe.

It may all seem a daunting task, particularly to plan whilst living on the other side of the world. But working through the problems logically should see it all through, although it may seem quite a relief when you finally head out of Yosemite Valley at the beginning of the long hike. You will very soon discover that it has all been worth it.

It is hoped that the information supplied in this guidebook will greatly assist walkers plan and achieve the JMT, truly a walk of a lifetime. Information of this type can get out of date quite quickly, so the author strongly advises prospective JMT hikers to check on as many details as possible before leaving for America. This is relatively easily done through

the Internet, and several of the more important web sites relevant to the JMT are included in this guide. Once on the Trail the best source of up-to-date information is other hikers, particularly those travelling in the opposite direction along the JMT, and various park rangers who will be encountered from time to time (a list of ranger stations is provided in Appendix 2).

WHICH DIRECTION?

Any long-distance path can, of course, be walked in either direction. So it is possible to walk the John Muir Trail either from south to north (Whitney to Yosemite) or from north to south (Yosemite to Whitney). Hikers walking the Pacific Crest Trail usually walk the JMT section of their route from south to north, as most PCT 'Thru-Hikers', for logistical reasons, travel

Mount Lyell, the highest peak in Yosemite, with its small glacier, towering above the head of Lyell Canyon (Day 5)

from Mexico to Canada. But for those walking only the John Muir Trail it is far better to hike the Trail from north to south.

If you travel from south to north, beginning at Whitney Portal, there are four major disadvantages. The very first stage is a climb of over 6000ft to the summit of Mount Whitney, at the seriously high altitude of 14,496ft. At this stage you will not be altitude acclimatised and so run a serious risk of suffering altitude sickness, which at best would severely affect your ability to continue northwards along the JMT. Secondly, there is no point along the route of the JMT between Whitney Portal and Muir Trail Ranch where further food supplies may be picked up, so the poorly acclimatised and unfit trail hiker would have to begin the walk by carrying a heavy load of 10 days' worth of food from the very beginning of the trek. Thirdly, the

southern half of the JMT passes through areas of total backcountry wilderness, where escape routes are relatively few and far apart (a list of escape routes is given in Appendix 3), and where even these usually require at least two and often more days to reach civilisation. So the most serious part of the Trail is encountered at the beginning of the trip when the overseas walker will be unused to the American wilderness and so less able to cope. Lastly, the southern section contains a half-dozen high mountain passes of over 10,000ft which come in quick succession, almost one per day. Again the walker not yet trail fit and altitude acclimatised will find the crossing of these high cols extremely arduous.

By walking from north to south, Yosemite to Whitney, all of these problems are overcome. The northern end of the Trail is at a much lower altitude than the southern half; compare the summit of Half Dome, 8836ft, with those of the 11,000ft+ passes further south and the 14,496ft of Mount Whitney itself. The climbs in the northern half of the Trail are generally not as long and hard as those further south, and altitude is gradually gained as the walker heads south, so allowing good acclimatisation. Furthermore, just three days (or even only two days if Half Dome is omitted) after leaving Yosemite Valley, Tuolumne Meadows on a main road is reached, where food supplies may be picked up and prepared foods purchased. Three and a half days later Reds Meadow is encountered, with

similar facilities. Then, 2½ days after that, comes the comfort and hospitality of Vermilion. And only two days later comes Muir Trail Ranch, which allows pre-posted food packages (see 'Posting food on ahead', below) to be collected. So there is less of a wilderness aspect on the northern half of the JMT compared to the southern half; the walker can therefore build up his or her trail fitness and experience of the Californian wilderness before tackling the harder, higher, wilder sections in the south.

For all these reasons the JMT hiker is strongly recommended to walk the

Shorter Routes Include:

- **JMT from Yosemite Valley to Tuolumne**, including the ascent of Half Dome. 3 days. There is a seasonal bus from Tuolumne Meadows back to Yosemite Valley at the end of this short but spectacular hike.

- **JMT from Yosemite or Tuolumne Meadows to Reds Meadow**, including Lyell Valley and the Devil's Postpile. 6½ or 3½ days. A seasonal shuttle bus can be used to exit the trail to the town of Mammoth Lakes at the end of this trek.

- **JMT from Yosemite or Tuolumne Meadows or Reds Meadow to Vermilion Valley Resort**. 2½, 6 or 9 days.

- **JMT from Yosemite or Tuolumne Meadows or Reds Meadow or Vermilion Resort to Muir Trail Ranch**. 2, 4½, 8 or 11 days. From Muir Trail Ranch there is a seasonal ferry across Florence Lake (or hike around it) to a roadhead. Hikers would then have to hitch a lift back to civilisation.

- **JMT from Vermilion Valley Resort or Muir Trail Ranch to Le Conte Canyon**, where the JMT can be left by a good trail over the Bishop Pass and so on to the town of Bishop: 5–7 days. Similarly, the JMT could be joined from Bishop by this route and then followed via Mount Whitney to Whitney Portal: 9–10 days.

Trail north to south, from Yosemite to Whitney. This is the direction described in this guidebook.

WHEN TO GO

The JMT is a high-level route over the High Sierras, mostly above 9000ft in altitude and often above 11,000ft. Very considerable quantities of snow fall on these mountains during the winter months. Snow remains on the high passes usually well into early summer. July is the first month of the year when the JMT could sensibly be considered, but in years of late spring snows it is likely that the higher sections of the Trail will still have a covering of snow, at least in the early days of that month. Melting snow also means swollen rivers, so an early summer crossing increases the risk of encountering difficult and dangerous river crossings.

The recommended month to hike the JMT is August, when the risk of lying snow and rivers in spate is at its lowest. Mosquitoes, which can be a menace in some areas, tend to be less of a nuisance later in the summer. The temperature even at the high altitudes of the High Sierras will probably be fairly high at this time of year (at least in the high 20s Celcius and probably well into the 30s), with some low temperatures at night (often at or below freezing), but with relatively low risk of severely low night-time temperatures. Precipitation, either rain or snow, will probably be very low.

However, violent thunderstorms with heavy rain, snow and hail can occur even during the summer months. This mountain range has one of the best climates of any high mountain area in the world, and most days during the summer months have blue skies and wall-to-wall sunshine.

The first week of September is also acceptable, but by mid-September some of the resorts and other facilities en route may be closing down, particularly if the weather starts deteriorating. However, September does have several advantages for experienced backpackers, including few mosquitoes, less traffic on the trail, ease of obtaining permits, autumn colours and fewer thunderstorms, but at the risk of freezing nights, a higher probability of snow and the stores (Reds Meadow and Vermilion) en route running down stock for the close of the season. By the end of September night-time temperatures are likely to plummet significantly, with the first heavy snows of the season at high altitude a very real possibility. By early October all the facilities on the JMT are closed, as winter begins to creep slowly into the High Sierras.

ALL OR PART OF THE TRAIL?

Overseas walkers are likely to spend a considerable sum of money travelling to the western United States and to invest a fair amount of time in planning the hike; they often wish, therefore, to attempt the whole of the

Breakfast in camp on the JMT

JMT. However, with time for food provisioning and other preparations, and travel to and from the trailheads, plus time for sightseeing in San Francisco and elsewhere, the total amount of time required to walk the whole of the JMT is at least four weeks.

Those who do not have this time available can still experience this most wonderful of mountain wilderness areas without committing to the whole of the JMT. Many of the logistical problems of food replenishment do not exist if a shorter section of the trail is envisaged. Most American hikers, in fact, usually hike only three to five days in the wilderness on any one occasion, usually entering JMT country along a side-trail and returning to a nearby roadhead or town by another side-trail. There is sufficient information in this guidebook to allow walkers to do this (see Appendix 3 – Escape Routes).

IN A GROUP OR ALONE?

The walker faces another important decision – whether to undertake the JMT as a member of a small group, with one other friend or spouse, or to go alone. There are benefits and disadvantages of either approach. Some authors and authorities strongly disapprove of walking alone, particularly in the wild and lonely areas of the world. Such disapproval arises mainly from the risk of accidents that could leave the solitary traveller unable to physically escape from the wilderness area or to summon assistance from others.

Entering a wilderness area, particularly a mountain environment, always entails a certain amount of risk, which will be greater if the individual travels alone. But, although the John Muir Trail passes through the heart of one of the largest wilderness areas in the United States, the individual will often encounter others along the trail, particularly during the main summer hiking season. The JMT hiker is merely following a narrow thread through the wilderness, rather than disappearing into the vast expanse all around him.

So if the lone walker suffers an accident it is quite likely that he or she will be found within a few hours, providing that the accident occurs along the route of the JMT. In this respect walking the JMT alone in the main holiday season is less hazardous than walking an unmarked route across the Scottish Highlands, for example. So lone walkers, whether from choice or from circumstance, shouldn't be deterred from attempting the JMT.

Hiking the Trail as part of a group has several advantages. Safety in numbers is one obvious one, as is companionship, but another significant benefit is load sharing. The solitary walker must carry all his equipment, whereas one stove, one tent, one guidebook, one map, one first-aid kit, etc, will suffice for two or three people. Hence the weight to be carried per person should be less when travelling in a group. Job sharing is another advantage of a group, from shopping and packaging of food prior to the trek to division of labour in camp, and so on.

The disadvantage of travelling with a group is that minor differences in personalities and preferences can be exacerbated by living a physically demanding, unfamiliar and sometimes uncomfortable lifestyle in close proximity to one another, with little time to retreat into one's own 'space'. One person may naturally walk faster than the others and so get tired and exasperated at constantly having to wait for the rest of the group. Some may like to stop frequently for botanising or taking photographs, whilst others prefer to push on. All such differences can be magnified during the sometimes stressful existence of life on the Trail and result in disagreements, arguments, feuds and general unpleasantness.

By going alone there are no such personality clashes, but other mental strains may replace those of the group. When alone there is no one else to provide moral, mental or physical support, and the almost inevitable lows whilst on a venture of this nature can seem much blacker without friendly support, comradeship and assistance. The state of being alone, a refreshing and often vitalising state, could descend into loneliness – a dispiriting, depressing experience. Fears over certain aspects of the trek, such as the possibility of a bear encounter, may prey more on the mind of a lone hiker.

In conclusion, there is no ideal way to walk the JMT. One must weigh the advantages and disadvantages of going alone or in a group. But whatever the final choice, walking the JMT is sure to be an experience of a lifetime.

WILDERNESS PERMITS

Before you set out on the John Muir Trail, or on any other hike that requires overnight camps in wilderness areas, you need to obtain a wilderness permit. **This is absolutely essential.** You will almost certainly encounter several park rangers while on your trek, and many of these will demand to see your permit. There are steep fines for venturing into the wilderness without a permit. National park rangers in the States hold much greater powers than national park wardens in the UK. Some have the power of arrest and, like the police, carry guns. They are usually extremely courteous and friendly, and can offer sound advice, but never think of crossing them or breaking the rules, which are in place

principally to protect this special but fragile environment. The system avoids overcrowding and reduces the impact on the wilderness areas.

There are strict allocations of permits, only a certain number being issued for each day from each trailhead. During the main holiday period during the summer months competition for them can be intense. Permits may be reserved up to 24 weeks in advance of the day you intend starting the Trail. You are strongly advised to make a request for a permit before making any other plans for walking the JMT. Once a permit has been reserved then it is safe to go ahead to book a flight to California and make all your other plans.

Generally hikers must leave their commencing trailhead (in this case

Looking eastwards towards the Mount Whitney massif from Guitar Lake (Day 19)

Horses kicking up the dust on the Trail in Lyell Canyon (Day 4)

Happy Isles, Yosemite Valley) on the day their permit begins. Make sure, therefore, that you allow yourself sufficient time after arriving in the States to buy all the food supplies needed for your hike, package them up and post them to various points along the Trail, and finally get yourself to Yosemite Village in time for the day your permit begins.

Make a reservation as early as possible – as soon as you are within 24 weeks of your planned starting date. Applying early is the best way of ensuring that you are granted your permit. Remember that a request for a permit reservation does not guarantee a reservation. If the quota for that day is full then you will be rejected. Give

an alternative starting date if possible.

You may request a reservation for a wilderness permit by one of three methods – by post, telephone or online (see below). If accepted you will receive a written confirmation, which will state the date of entry to the wilderness area, the trailhead where your hike will begin and the number in your party. Retain this as proof of your reservation to present at the Wilderness Centre in Yosemite Village when you arrive. You will then receive your permit. Keep it safe at all times on the JMT and show it to any ranger who requests to inspect it.

The conditions and procedures for making permit reservations do change from time to time, and it is essential to ascertain the current situation by looking on the web or by telephoning the Wilderness Centre in Yosemite. When doing this or making a reservation by phone do not forget the significant time difference between Europe and California (see 'Time in California' under 'Walking the Trail', below).

If you are walking the JMT as described in this guidebook you will enter the wilderness area at Yosemite. You therefore need to obtain a permit from the Yosemite end of the Trail (the application procedures described in full below apply to Yosemite). The Yosemite Association, a non profit making organisation, is now responsible for issuing permits at Yosemite.

If you wish to hike the JMT from south to north (Whitney to Yosemite) you need to obtain a permit from the Whitney end of the Trail, as it is from here that you will be entering the wilderness area. For information check out the website of the Inyo Forest Wilderness Reservation Service (www. fs.fed.us/r5/inyo), the private contractor that now deals with wilderness permit applications on behalf of the Inyo National Forest. Click onto 'Passes & Permits' and go to 'Wilderness Permits'. Note that in order to cope with the large and increasing numbers of walkers wanting to climb Mount Whitney, permits are required not only for overnight wilderness campers but also for day hikers in the Whitney area above Lone Pine Lake. (Permits are limited to 150 day hikers and 50 overnighters – fines of up to $200 are levied on anyone found without a permit in the Whitney area.)

Making a Permit Reservation by Phone

A phone call to the States is perhaps the best way to ensure that you obtain the right permit for the right day; you will be told immediately of any problems and can discuss alternative dates. Provided you have all the necessary information to hand, it should take only a few minutes to make your reservation.

TREKKING PERMITS

The whole concept of trekking permits is alien to the British and European way of managing wilderness areas, and imposes restrictions on freedoms which elsewhere are considered to be fundamental rights. Do remember, however, that America has much greater areas of unspoilt wilderness than the Old World, and its conservation of these areas is to be congratulated. Restricting and controlling the numbers of humans allowed into the wilderness areas of its national parks has done much to protect and preserve these mountain wonderlands for future generations. As a guest in the US, do respect their way of doing things. Be patient and tolerant of the permit system.

The telephone number of the Wilderness Centre in Yosemite is: (209) 372 0740 (preceded by the international code for the US, 001 from the UK). The number is often very busy, so persistence may be required. The office is normally open between 8am and 4.30pm Pacific Time. You will need to give the following information.

- Your name, address and daytime telephone number.
- The exact starting and finishing dates of your trek (be sure to allow yourself a sufficient number of days for the JMT; if you request too few days then there may be problems if your permit runs out before you reach the end of the Trail).
- The starting and ending trailhead (Happy Isles, Yosemite Valley and Whitney Portal). It is important to state that you are going to be walking the John Muir Trail in its entirety. There are considerable restrictions on entry into the Mount Whitney area and usually your permit must carry a special stamp to allow you entry into this area along the JMT. Be sure to confirm the current regulations regarding this and any other special conditions along the route.
- The number of people in your group (you will not normally be asked details about the others in your group, but it is best to have these on hand when you make the call just in case). The maximum size of each group is normally 15 persons.

You will also need details of your credit card to hand as there is a small administrative charge (currently $5 per person in the group) for making the reservation.

Once the reservation is made, written confirmation will be sent by post. You will receive a permit for the group, not separate permits for each individual within your group, although if walking alone your 'group size' will be one person.

Making a Permit Reservation by Post

Provide the same information as above in your letter, which should be addressed to Wilderness Reservations, Yosemite Association, PO Box 545, Yosemite, CA 95389, US. A method of payment will be required, so enclose your credit card number.

This method of application is not recommended for those outside the US, as it is very time consuming, particularly if there are any problems. Permits are quickly allocated, and you may end up without a permit or with a permit several days or even weeks after you actually wanted it.

If you do decide on this method of application it is important that your written request arrives at least 24 weeks prior to the date you wish to start the trek. Although, if it arrives earlier it will not be processed until 24 weeks before the first day of the planned hike.

View south from Forester Pass of two large unnamed lakes (Day 18)

org/visitor/wild.html). Read the information on this page and fill in the online reservation form. You will need to give a credit card number to pay your reservation fee, but it is a secure site. The availability of permits for various park trailheads can also be checked out on this website.

Up to 60% of wilderness permits are issued in advance. The remaining 40% are issued in person at the trailhead issuing stations (in this case the Wilderness Center in Yosemite Village) on a first-come, first-served basis on the day of, or one day before, the beginning of the hike. You are strongly advised not to risk obtaining a wilderness

Making a Permit Reservation Online

This does not have the delay problems associated with 'snail mail', but you have no opportunity to ask any questions about availability, etc. To make an online reservation check out www.yosemite.org (the Yosemite Park Association's website called 'Yosemite Online'). Click onto 'Visitor Information' and then onto 'Wilderness Page' (www.yosemite.

permit in this way. To fly all the way to California and then not be able to walk the Trail because of an inability to obtain a wilderness permit would be unfortunate, to say the least.

Finally, if disaster strikes after you have made your permit reservations and you cannot hike the JMT, contact the reservation service to cancel your permit. If you neglect to do this you will be preventing other hikers from enjoying this magnificent wilderness.

Note for 2010 Reprint: The experience of some hikers suggests that emailing the Wilderness Centre with a permit request might be the easiest way of securing a permit. Apparently the Wilderness Centre process permit emails only once a day, as soon as the office opens in the morning, when permit requests are dealt with on a first-come, first-served basis. It is always advisable to check the website before making a permit request to ascertain the current situation with regard to permits.

A Yosemite permit reservation can be made up to 24 weeks (168 days), but no later than two days, in advance of your start date, but you are **strongly** recommended to obtain a permit as early as possible. The National Parks Service has a website showing the dates that are fully allocated for permits: www.nps.gov/yose/rptFullTrailhead Dates.htm. The price for a wilderness permit was $5 in 2008. Backpacking the JMT from north-to-south (as in this guidebook) automatically includes a permit for Mount Whitney, but if the walk is made from south to north, then an additional fee of $15 may be levied for the ascent of Whitney.

Note that permits are also issued at Happy Valley, and may be available there if the Yosemite ones have all been issued.

It is advisable to pick up your permit from the Rangers' Office the afternoon before you plan to set out on your hike.

FLIGHTS TO CALIFORNIA

The nearest major international airport to the northern terminus of the John Muir Trail at Yosemite is San Francisco; however Lone Pine, the town nearest to Whitney Portal, at the end of the Trail, is closer to Los Angeles than to San Francisco. The best airline ticket to purchase is therefore an 'open-jaw' ticket inward to San Francisco and outward from Los Angeles. Such tickets are often no more expensive than buying a return from the airport of entry.

Many of the major European and American carriers fly from London to San Francisco and LA. It is just a matter of getting the best deal on flights. Good deals are often to be had by booking on the internet. It is advisable to make a booking several months in advance, as the optimum time to walk the JMT coincides with the main summer holiday season, when there is likely to be greatest demand for trans-Atlantic flights and prices are liable to be high.

There are airport buses from San Francisco International Airport into the centre of the city, and similarly ample public transport in Los Angeles to the international airport.

PUBLIC TRANSPORT TO AND FROM THE TRAILHEAD

For the most technologically advanced nation in the world the United States of America has a limited public transport system, and there is little provision for the few who do not have cars. This is not good news for foreign long-distance hikers who visit the States. Hiring a car is not practical for JMT walkers, except possibly at the end of the hike, provided that the hire company agrees to let you drop the car off at Los Angeles airport prior to your departure. As overseas JMT walkers are likely to fly into San Francisco and out of Los Angeles, they will need to travel from San Francisco to Yosemite Valley for the start of the Trail, and at the end to travel to Los Angeles for the homeward flight. The former journey is relatively easy by public transport, but the latter much less so. Both are described below.

To the Trailhead: San Francisco to Yosemite Valley via Merced

There is a Greyhound bus service that runs from San Francisco to Merced.

Alternatively, it is a relatively straight-forward journey by bus and train from San Francisco to Yosemite Valley via the town of Merced. Not only that, but the super Amtrak double-decker train ride between Emeryville and Merced is likely to be one of the highlights of your time in the States.

The journey is split into three sections: from San Francisco to Emeryville by bus; by train from Emeryville to Merced; and by bus from Merced to Yosemite Valley. It is recommended that the first two sections of the journey are taken in succession (the bus and train timetables are co-ordinated for these two parts of the journey), but that the journey is then broken in Merced for a couple of overnights there. This will allow time for buying provisions for the trip and packaging and posting them to various pick-up points further along the Trail.

Rock towers seen at close hand on the ascent to Forester Pass (Day 18)

The information below was correct at the time of writing, and will give sufficient information to allow initial planning, but services may change, so up-to-date information should always be sought. Check out timetables at www.amtrak.com (this site includes details of both train and connecting buses for the entire journey between San Francisco and Yosemite Valley). Note that the 24-hour clock is not generally used for timetables in the US. The information below refers to the summer season only.

San Francisco to Emeryville: The bus leaves from a number of points in San Francisco, so choose the one nearest your hotel: San Francisco Moscone Center (SFM), San Francisco Financial Center (SFF), San Francisco Ferry Building (SFC), San Francisco Fisherman's Wharf (SFW), San Francisco Union Square (SFS) and San Francisco Peninsula Line (SFP). There are three buses daily, bus 6614 in the morning, bus 6616 at lunchtime and bus 6618 in the afternoon. The journey time to Emeryville is approximately 55mins. Luggage is checked in at the bus station for the whole journey by bus and train to Merced. There may be a surcharge for any rucksack weighing more than 23kg. The bus travels to Emeryville train station for the connection to Merced.

Emeryville to Merced: Three trains a day connect with the above buses: the 714 train connects with the 6614

bus in the morning, the 716 train connects with the 6616 bus at lunchtime, and the 718 train connects with the 6618 bus in the afternoon. Journey time is about 2hrs 45mins. To give one example: if the 9.15am bus from San Francisco Fisherman's Wharf is taken then this will arrive at Emeryville train station at 10.05am in time for the 10.15am train to Merced, arriving at 12.50pm.

Merced to Yosemite Valley: At the time of writing there are three buses per day between Merced and Yosemite Valley, two in the morning (buses 8402 and 8412) and one in the late afternoon (bus 8416). Journey time is between 2hrs 20mins and 2hrs 50mins. Buses leave from Merced railway station, connecting with the train services (see Amtrak website). It is possible by taking the first bus of the day from San Francisco to be in Yosemite Valley by early afternoon, to collect your permit and so set out on the JMT early the next morning. When arriving by bus at Yosemite, ask to be put off at the Visitor Center in Yosemite Village, which is close to the Wilderness Center, where you must first go to pick up your wilderness permits.

At the time of writing The Travel Bureau in Wombourne (see Appendix 6) is the UK agent for Amtrak in the US and will take bookings for the bus/ train/bus journey from San Francisco to Yosemite Valley.

From the Trailhead:
Lone Pine to Los Angeles

Once you have completed the JMT you will have to reach Lone Pine, 13 miles from the end of the Trail at Whitney Portal (for hints on how best to achieve this see the end of Day 21, below). No doubt you will wish to spend a night or two in Lone Pine before moving on to Los Angeles for your return journey. This will allow you some time to sort out your onward travel arrangements. At the time of writing there is no public transport service between Lone Pine and Los Angeles. Unfortunately, due to scarcity of passengers the Greyhound bus service on this route ceased in 2001. This is a major snag for all walkers of the JMT. At the time of writing there are no Greyhound bus services from either Ridgecrest or Bishop to LA.

Some American hikers will no doubt have friends or relatives picking them up at Lone Pine, and if you have become friendly with them they may just offer you a lift. If you can get a lift as far south as Lancaster then there you could pick up a Greyhound bus to LA (two services daily, morning and late afternoon, 2hrs 25mins for the journey), but unfortunately Lancaster is nearly three-quarters of the distance between Lone Pine and Los Angeles.

There were plans to create a bus service from Lone Pine to Ridgecrest, a town further south and about a third of the distance to LA. If this is operating by the time of your visit then it would be possible to go by bus to Ridgecrest, from where a vehicle could be hired to take you to LA and its airport. Another option would be to hitch north to Bishop, from where a car could be hired from a company that would hopefully allow you to drop off the car at the LA airport.

None of these alternatives is ideal, but you will not be the only hiker in difficulty. Those with at least four in their party could hire a taxi or small minibus to Los Angeles. The fare would not be exorbitant if shared among several people. Be sure to shop around to get the best deal. If you have been hiking alone or with a spouse or one friend then try to join up with a few other hikers who are also looking for transport to LA, or at least in that general direction. The cost of hiring transport can then be shared.

However you leave Lone Pine you will be sure to manage it somehow! The problem will probably not seem too great, as you have just completed one of the great treks of the world, and life will be looking just fine!

Note for 20010 Reprint: Since the original research was undertaken for this guidebook several hikers have reported that no difficulty should be encountered in hitching a lift from Whitney Portal to Lone Pine. There are now three buses a week (Monday/Wednesday/Friday) from Lone Pine to Ridgecrest, further down the Owens Valley. This bus connects with the train that runs north to San Francisco, or alternatively one-way car hire should be available from Ridgecrest

(Avis, Dollar or Enterprise). It is also possible to take a bus from Ridgecrest to Bakersfield (although this might involve an overnight stay to make the connection) and then the train.

Another alternative is to catch a bus from Lone Pine to Bishop (three buses every day, Inyo Mono Transit or Eastern Sierra Transit), followed by a bus to Reno the next day, and finally a train to San Francisco (or one of the several other options from Reno, bus, hire- car or plane. Note that the Bishop to Reno bus operates only three times per week, on Tuesday, Thursday and Friday and that a reservation is strongly advised, for example by phoning from Whitney Portal Store. The Lone Pine to Ridgecrest, the Lone Pine to Bishop and the Bishop to Reno bus services are all operated by Inyo Mono Transit (see http://county ofinyo.org/transit/transit.htm).

Another option at Bishop, for those wishing to return to the Yosemite area, is to sleep overnight at El Rancho Motel (near the bus stops) and next day take the early morning Eastern Sierra Transit bus (operates Monday, Tuesday, Thursday and Friday) to Lee Vining. From there, the Yarts bus leaves from Lee Vining Tioga Mobil Gas Mart for Tuolumne Meadows and on to Yosemite Valley.

Remember that any of these services may be withdrawn or significantly changed at any time, and that other possibilities may present themselves in the future. Use the Trail grapevine to keep abreast of the current situation.

For other possibilities check out the useful website: http://alumnus.caltech.edu/~rbell/JMTTransport.html.gz.

BOOKING ACCOMMODATION

Consider booking accommodation in San Francisco for your first night in the US. It is advisable to do this from home before arriving in the States, as you will probably be arriving in the middle of the summer holiday period when most accommodation will be full. A booking in one of the more upmarket hotels in San Francisco can be made via the internet. The net is less useful for cheap and cheerful hotels, in which a booking is more likely to be secured by arriving in person, but this is not advisable if your flight arrives fairly late in the day.

Unfortunately, most flights from Europe arrive in the late afternoon or early evening, when passengers will feel extremely jet-lagged. (Remember that Californian time is 8 hours behind the UK.) San Francisco has two youth hostels, one in Union Square in Downtown and the other in the popular Fisherman's Wharf area of the town (Fort Mason – the bus stop to Yosemite is a 25-minute walk from this hostel and a good supermarket is only two minutes' walk away).

Booking is strongly advised for visits in the main summer holiday season (Hostelling International, 312 Mason St, San Francisco, CA 94102 (sfdowntown @norcalhostels.org) and Hostelling International, Fort Mason, Building

240, San Francisco, CA 94123 (sfhostel@norcal hostels.org)). The San Francisco hostels can also be booked on the Hostelling International website.

The best form of accommodation in Merced is a motel room. This can be booked easily for the major chain motels (such as the Best Western in Merced) over the Internet, but again it seems to be more difficult to book a motel room at the cheaper end of the market over the net.

Several hikers have recommended the Yosemite Bug Lodge (www.yosemitebug. com) a HI hostel situated about 25 miles from Yosemite village and on the bus route from Merced to Yosemite (bus stop, outside the entrance). Accommodation is in dormitories, tent cabins or wooden cabins and a fresh food café is on site. The bus fare from the hostel to Yosemite is $12, and this is said to include the $10 Park entrance fee! (2010 prices).

On arrival at Yosemite Village you will probably head for the Backpackers' Campsite, which is a

A view of the Lyell Fork river in the Lyell Canyon (Day 4)

5–10 minute walk from North Pines/ Stables bus stop number 18. Only people with wilderness permits can camp here. Alternatively you can stay overnight in the other forms of accommodation at Yosemite Village, such as the lodges. Details of these and booking information can be obtained from the park offices in Yosemite Village.

Accommodation will probably be required at Lone Pine at the end of the JMT and also in LA (fairly close to the airport if possible) the night before your flight home. As you may not be able to predict the day that you will finish the JMT and so arrive in Lone Pine, it is not advisable to pre-book accommodation there (and it is always possible that you will not finish the Trail and so need accommodation at a different location).

Those walking the JMT in August will arrive in Lone Pine at the end of that month, when many Americans have finished their annual holidays and pressure on motel rooms is not as intense. There are several motels to choose from in Lone Pine. The Best Western is ½ mile south of town, and the Dow Villa Motel (PO Box 205, 310 South Main Street, Lone Pine, CA 93545. Reservations 800-824-9317. dowvilla@qnet.com) is recommended.

MAPS

There are several maps that cover all or part of the John Muir Trail. The United States Forestry Service produces a number of 'Wilderness Maps' which are useful, covering the JMT outside Yosemite. The John Muir/Sequoia–Kings Canyon Wilderness Map and the Ansel Adams Wilderness Map are the most useful sheets.

There are several maps available locally which cover the Yosemite National Park. The Inyo National Forest Map is another possible map, and covers the whole area through which the Trail passes. These maps are easily obtainable in the US, but less so outside the country.

The best maps both for planning in the UK and use on the JMT in America are contained within the *John Muir Trail Map-Pack: Tom Harrison's Maps*. The Map-Pack consists of 13 colour topographical, shaded-relief maps depicting the John Muir Trail, the Pacific Crest Trail and numerous side-trails. Campgrounds, ranger stations and information centres are also shown. The maps run from Whitney to Yosemite Valley (sheet numbers 1 to 13), so walkers following the route in this guidebook will use them in the order Sheet 13 to Sheet 1. The sheets required for each stage of the hike are given at the beginning of each daily stage in the route guide section of this book. For further information on Tom Harrison's maps go to www.tomharrisonmaps.com.

Tom Harrison's *John Muir Trail Map-Pack* is usually obtainable in Britain from retailers such as The Map Shop in Upton-upon-Severn and Stanford's in London, Bristol and Manchester (see Appendix 6). The Map-Pack is rather expensive, particularly when purchased in the UK, but it is the author's recommended map for the JMT. The maps are clear and easy to use – although the contour lines are at 80ft intervals.

Navigation along the John Muir Trail is generally easy, far more so than a route across the Scottish Highlands, for example, and more straightforward than many long-distance routes in Europe. With use of the Tom Harrison maps and this guidebook the trail of the JMT should never be in doubt.

EQUIPMENT

The importance of packing light for the John Muir Trail cannot be over-stressed. The experienced and inexperienced backpacker can usually be differentiated by the much lighter load carried by the former. The inexperienced tends not to know which items of kit are essential and which can be omitted without compromising either safety or comfort.

Assemble the gear that you think you need for the trip and then try to be ruthless in discarding items that are not really necessary, or replace them with lighter alternatives. Limit yourself to a very small number of luxury (non-essential) items. The American guru of ultra-lightweight wilderness backpacking is Ray Jardine, a man who has probably walked the Pacific Crest Trail more times than anyone else. His philosophy and tips for load lightening can be found in *The Pacific Crest Trail Hiker's Handbook* (see Appendix 7 – Bibliography).

Generally, gear must be selected to cope with a hot, dry climate (it is assumed here that you are travelling the JMT during the high summer season).

Banner Peak and Mount Ritter seen from Island Pass (Day 5)

Footwear

Lightweight fabric boots are the recommended footwear. There is little need for expensive waterproof material, as precipitation will probably be low, and the underfoot conditions are generally dry and dusty. Likewise, heavy leather boots are unnecessary. It is sometimes said that an extra 1lb on the foot is equivalent to an extra 10lbs on the back, so lightweight boots will reduce fatigue considerably. Ensure that the boots are well worn in before leaving to walk the JMT. Short lightweight gaiters are useful in preventing small stones from entering footwear, a frequent problem on the often dry and dusty trail.

Some form of lightweight shoe, for example a good-quality walking sandal with good tread, is advisable for use in San Francisco/Merced before the start of the trek and in Lone Pine/Los Angeles at the end. Sandals are also useful when making river crossings, ensuring that your boots remain dry. The ability to change into some form of comfortable alternative footwear at the end of the each day on the Trail also provides a thankful rest for hot and tired feet.

Banner Peak and Mount Ritter (Day 6)

Backpack

The backpacker's most important item of gear is undoubtedly the backpack itself. A good-quality, ergonomically designed modern backpack, which transfers much of the weight of the pack off the back and onto the hips, is essential. A capacity of at least 70 litres is recommended. Whether side pockets are included or not is a matter of personal preference, but remember that considerable quantities of water

50

will have to be carried, and up to 10 days' worth of food, so the sac needs to be versatile and capable of carrying a reasonably high weight and volume. A well-padded hip belt is essential, and most modern sacs also offer a chest strap. Do not take a backpack that you have not previously used on trips of at least four to five days' duration. Any problems or discomforts with the pack should by then be evident.

Clothing

The layer principle should be used. For a base layer a wicking T-shirt or equivalent garment is the best item of clothing. A good-quality fleece for the mid-layer and a breathable water-proof and windproof outer garment should complete the clothing system. Lightweight shorts will almost cer-tainly be worn most days while on the trek, but a pair of lightweight trousers is also required, not only for evening use and for travelling to and from the States, but also if and when weather conditions deteriorate.

It is also essential to take along wet-weather gear, as fierce rain and snow storms are not uncommon even in summer, as well as a warm jacket/fleece and a lightweight pair of gloves. Temperatures in high alti-tudes can plummet to well below freezing during bad weather and par-ticularly at night.

Tent

American hikers generally use lighter and less robust tents than their northern European counterparts because of the much drier conditions in areas such as California. Often a tarp (suspended outer rain covering) or shelters (similar but somewhat more substantial that the tarp) are used in the US instead of the conventional backpacking tent with inner and outer compartments. Tarps and shelters are generally lighter than conventional backpacking tents, but most British backpackers, unless they envisage frequent visits to the US, may not wish to invest in an American-style tent or shelter. Those who do should look at the range of shelters sold by the Golite Company.

A sturdy but lightweight moun-tain tent is recommended for the JMT. When the nights are warm and precipitation extremely unlikely some hikers may prefer to erect only the inner tent, if possible with their tent system. However, very violent storms can occur, and during such an event the backpacker protected only with a simple, less than stable tent or shelter would be extremely vulnerable. An alternative to a tent would be a good quality Gore-Tex bivvy bag, as these are very lightweight, and a sleeping bag. Many nights could be spent out in the open using only a sleeping bag, with the bivvy bag being used only on very cold nights or if there was the like-lihood of rain.

Sleeping Bag

The sleeping bag you take needs to be lightweight, but capable of coping with temperatures as low as -10°C. Down feather is recommended, as these pack down to smaller sizes than an equivalent synthetic bag. As the climate is generally dry, they are unlikely to get soaked with water, the only factor which greatly affects a down bag.

Camping Mat or Lightweight Inflatable Mattress

Either a mat or mattress is acceptable, but the thermal backpacking inflatable airbed provides much more comfort and protection from the hard ground (but has the disadvantage that if punctured and therefore useless, would be impossible to replace on a trek such as the JMT – a repair kit is an essential item of kit if carrying an inflatable mat). A closed-cell insulating mat is lighter and cheaper, but bulkier to carry.

Camping Stove

You are strongly advised to use a stove for cooking along the JMT, rather than relying on open fires, which are unreliable, environmentally damaging and are banned above certain altitudes in the various parks and wilderness areas along the Trail (see 'Low-impact trekking and national park/wilderness regulations', below).

The stove of choice for the States is the MSR stove, a versatile multifuel stove which uses white gasoline (Shellite), petrol or standard kerosene. It works at high pressure with a very hot flame, so water boils rapidly.

An added convenience is that fuel for these stoves is readily available throughout the US and in the stores along the JMT at Tuolumne Meadows, Reds Meadow, Vermilion and Muir Trail Ranch.

The adjustable MSR Dragonfly stove is highly recommended. The disadvantage of these stoves is that they are very expensive to purchase in the UK (much cheaper in the States) and that they take some practice to use properly. Impurities in fuel can sometimes lead to a blockage of the stove's jets, so it is advisable to take along the appropriate cleaning tools and know how to quickly remove a blockage. They are also quite noisy. Some lightweight campers prefer the MSR Whisperlite Internationale, which is lighter than the MSR Dragonfly and also multi-fuel, but its flame is non-adjustable.

There are two other alternatives: the Trangia-type stove, which burns methylated spirits or methanol and is very stable and simple to use, or a camping-gas-style stove. The main disadvantage of these cookers is a possible lack of the appropriate fuel along the JMT. In 2005 it was reported by several British trekkers that 'Epigas' butane/propane canisters are now widely available along the Trail, although Muir Trail Ranch is not a reliable supplier of canister gas (it does promise that white gas for liquid fuel stoves is always in stock). Gas stoves are less heavy than the MSR type stove, and modern ones have overcome the problem of loss of pressure when half empty and the difficulty of operation at low air temperatures.

Remember that you are prohibited from taking any type of fuel on board an aircraft, so all fuel for the trip must be purchased in the US, and any unused fuel disposed of with care before the return journey.

Lead muleteer carrying trekkers' provisions along the JMT

Cooking Equipment

Do not take plates, bowls and forks as none of these items are necessary, but are merely additional weight and bulk in the backpack. A spoon is adequate to eat the dehydrated meals that form the basis of a hiker's diet while on the Trail. Food can be eaten out of the cooking pot or, in the case of some specialised backpacking foods, straight out of the packet. One lightweight cooking pot per person should suffice, although an extra pot can come in handy. A plastic mug is essential for drinks and soup, a recommended starter for your evening meal. A Swiss army knife or equivalent provides several tools, including a sharp knife, a pair of scissors, a can opener and corkscrew, although the latter implements will only be needed when canned food or a bottle of wine is bought at one of the stores en route. A lighter is more convenient to use than matches.

Water Filter and Water Bottles

A good-quality water filter is strongly recommended when hiking in the US. One should be enough to filter water for 3–4 people. Alternatively, a

FIRST AID KIT

A first aid kit is an essential item for JMT hikers to include in their back-packs. Several commercial packs are available, but those compiling their own kits should consider including at least the following items.

- aspirin, paracetamol or other pain killers
- antiseptic cream
- anti-diarrhoea tablets (Imodium or Lomotil), antibiotics, gastric antac-ids, salt tablets
- oral rehydration salts (eg. Dioralyte)
- metronidazole (Flagyl) for the treatment of giardiasis
- sterile dressings of medium and large sizes, sterile eye pads, trian-gular bandages, disposable gloves, crepe roller bandages
- cleansing wipes
- adhesive tape
- scissors (if not available as part of a Swiss army knife)
- safety pins
- mole skin, second skin or equivalent (for blisters)
- mycota powder (for athlete's foot sufferers)
- insect repellent
- plasters of various shapes and sizes

Although not a first aid item, one vitamin/mineral pill per day for the dura-tion of the trek will prevent any possible deficiency.

It is a good idea before setting out for America to check that your polio and tetanus inoculations are up to date.

considerable number of water purify-ing tablets, or equivalent, must be car-ried, capable of killing protozoan as well as bacterial pathogens (see 'Water purification' under 'Walking the Trail', below). You need one or two water containers, with capacity such that you can carry up to two litres a person.

Some water bottles are designed to be compatible with particular types

of water filters on the market, such that the tube from the water filter feeds directly into the water bottle in a water-tight manner. These are the recommended form of water carrier for those using a water filter.

Dehydration is a constant threat in the hot temperatures and high alti-tudes of the Sierra Nevada. If a water container is stored away in a backpack then considerable effort is required to take off the pack each time a drink is required, and the hiker may take in insufficient liquid. Some water bottles are designed to fit on the hip belt of a backpack, so providing easy access to water. Water is even more conveniently supplied to the walker by use of a 'Platypus' or equivalent system, which delivers water via a mouth siphon tube from a reservoir held in the backpack. As it is so important to drink sufficient quantities of water on this Trail walkers should consider using such a device to deliver water frequently to the body.

Compass/GPS/Altimeter

Navigation is rarely a serious problem on the JMT, but do not neglect to take a compass. A GPS may be useful, but is not essential for walkers competent in the use of map and compass. Similarly an altimeter/barometer would be a useful, but certainly not essential, tool.

If you do take an altimeter then it is a good idea to adjust the instrument to operate in feet before you leave for the States. US maps are not metric, and the procedure for changing from metres to feet can be quite complicated on some models, requiring reference to the manual, which one would obviously not wish to carry on the trek.

Trekking Poles

The extra weight of carrying trekking poles is more than justified when backpacking a steep mountain trail such as the JMT. The added support and stability they provide, particularly when carrying a heavy pack, and the stress and strain they save on knee and hip joints will greatly benefit the hiker over the period on the Trail.

First Aid Kit

Walkers on the JMT are often several days from outside help, so a good first aid kit is essential (see 'First aid kit' box, above, and 'Health and medical considerations' under 'Walking the Trail').

Sun Protection

High-factor sunscreen, factor 35 or above, is essential for trekking in California. Lipsalve will help prevent cracked and chapped lips. Sunglasses are a must, preferably with UV Polaroid lenses. A sunhat will probably be required on most days.

Camera/Binoculars

A camera is a must for most people. If you normally use an SLR camera with detachable lenses then do take account of the significant weight of this equipment and perhaps consider taking a good-quality compact camera instead. Be sure to take sufficient film to last the duration of the trip.

Binoculars are important for bird and animal watchers, but are also useful for searching out the route ahead. There are excellent small and lightweight binoculars on the market.

Torch

During August night falls around 8–9pm, so it is likely that you will be spending some time each evening sitting around camp, stargazing, before retiring for the night. A torch with spare batteries is therefore advisable. A headtorch is preferable in camp as it leaves the hands free for jobs such as cooking and washing up – a very lightweight LED headtorch is ideal. Remember that Americans use the term 'flashlight' for what the British call a torch. It is inadvisable to tell a customs' officer that you are carrying a torch as you are likely to be whisked away and searched for an acetylene blowtorch, or the like!

Sewing Kit/Repair Kits

Any emergency repairs to clothing will have to be done en route. A very small sewing kit (a needle and a few appropriate threads) should be adequate. Small repair kits for tents, sleeping mats and the like are recommended, as is a tiny tube of superglue (could be essential if the sole of your boot decides to part company with the upper). A short length of light plastic string is also invaluable (for small repair jobs and for hanging washing up to dry).

Detergent/Towel/Bowl

Do not take soap and/or non-biodegradable detergents (see 'Low-impact trekking and national park/wilderness regulations', below). A small, lightweight backpacking towel is much lighter than a conventional towel. A small collapsible, plastic bowl weighs very little and is extremely useful for carrying water for the washing of pans, items of clothes and oneself. Water can then easily be disposed well away from water sources.

Food always heads the list of concerns while hiking the JMT: getting enough of it, carrying it, and protecting it from theft by Black Bears. It is essential to plan in advance both your food requirements and where to obtain supplies, as much of your food will have to be purchased in the States (see 'Buying food for the JMT', below). As it is not advisable to carry supplies for the entire Trail, food then has to be packaged and posted on to various pick-up points along the route (see 'Posting food on ahead', below).

Because hikers have to carry food supplies in their backpack, the basis of any backcountry diet will be dehydrated food. This may play havoc with you intestinal system, but it is only for a three week period – less, in fact, with the fresh and cooked food that can be purchased in Tuolumne Meadows, Reds Meadow Resort and Vermilion Valley Resort en route to supplement your diet.

Consideration must be given as to where to buy your foodstuffs. Unless you are in the US for several weeks before setting out on the JMT, the time between arriving in the US and leaving for the Trail is critical for buying food-stuffs for the whole of the JMT. If you wish to take specialist prepared back-packing foods you may have to obtain these in the States when you arrive, which will take time.

For this reason you may wish to purchase part of your food supplies in Britain and take them with you to the States. However, there are restrictions on the type of foodstuffs that can be imported into the United States, in particular meat, dairy and fruit products. Don't assume that just because food is dehydrated it will be permitted. The penalties for attempting to bring illegal foodstuffs into the US are severe, and up-to-date regulations can be obtained from the American Embassy in London (see Appendix 6).

Specialist dehydrated backpacking meals are available in the UK from various companies, such as Raven Foods and Expedition Foods. In the States Adventure Foods can be recommended (see Appendix 6) as can Mountain House freeze-dried meals. Such meals tend to be rather expensive, so it is worth trying to obtain a discount if buying in bulk. The number of calories provided by each course is normally given on the packet, and this is important when planning to ensure that sufficient calories are consumed each day. The main consideration is to take foods with the highest calorific value per unit weight. Remember that your lifestyle while on the Trail will be extremely active: eat accordingly. Note that most commercially packaged

dehydrated foods are calibrated for an altitude of 5000ft. At 10,000ft, the height of many camps on the JMT, the boiling point of water is lower, and the packet instructions will therefore probably lead to undercooked food. Hence after pouring in boiling water and resealing, wrap the foil bag in a fleece, and leave for at least 50% longer than the time indicated on the packet.

Variety, too, is important to ensure that sufficient nutrients of all types are consumed and to prevent your palette from becoming jaded. It is almost as important to take foodstuffs that you actually like to eat! And try to plan for the unexpected. Be sure to carry some spare food in

Sorting out daily food rations in a US motel room prior to leaving for Yosemite

TIPS FOR TRAIL FOODS

- For breakfast, muesli with nuts mixed with milk powder makes a good meal.
- It is important to supplement   specialised dehydrated backpacking foods with sufficient quantities of pasta, rice, cous-cous or dehydrated potato.
- A daily vitamin tablet will prevent any shortfall of vitamins or minerals.
- Bread soon goes stale and becomes inedible. Dried biscuits, crispbread or oatcakes are good substitutes, but are easily crushed in an over-full backpack. Tortillas are another good bread alternative, available also in wholemeal; they are long lasting, and are delicious and filling when served, for example, with peanut butter or tuna.
- Muesli and other high-energy bars are light to carry, and do not form a sticky mess like chocolate in high temperatures.
- Don't forget tea bags and/or instant coffee.

case adverse weather, injury, illness or any other problem that causes a delay on the Trail.

Remember too that when buying food it is important to consider not just calories and weight but also volume, as you will have to carry the food, probably in a bear barrel of limited size, and sending food caches to Muir Trail Ranch is expensive, so it is sensible to keep the number of food-containing plastic buckets sent there to a minimum. Peanut butter has good calories per ounce, but is also compact for fitting into a bear barrel, whereas cracker biscuits, for example, although having good calories per ounce, are of less use as they take up a lot of space. With dried foodstuffs, more or less whatever their composition, 2lb per person per day is the minimum.

And when you have chosen and bought your food supplies for the JMT your work is not over. Sort out the food into daily quantities of breakfast, lunch and dinner; pack away in your backpack the food for the first days on the trail; and package the rest of it for despatch to various points along the Trail (see 'Posting food on ahead', below).

Buying food for the JMT

Whether or not you take some dehydrated foodstuffs into the States (see 'Planning food supplies' above) it will be necessary to purchase the bulk of your supplies in America. The recommended point of entry is San Francisco, and from here you will travel to Merced prior to taking a bus into Yosemite. There is a limited range of food in Yosemite, but certainly not enough for the whole trek. Food for the Trail must therefore be purchased either in San Francisco or Merced.

San Francisco has many large supermarkets as well as outlets selling specialised backpacking foods, so it is quite feasible to stock up on supplies here. Supermarkets tend to be found in the suburbs, so locating them is not easy, nor is finding transport from your hotel to the supermarket and back again. However, there is a large and well-stocked Safeway supermarket within a short walking distance of Fisherman's Wharf. This is particularly convenient for those staying at the Downtown HI hostel in Mason Street (recommended by several JMT hikers). Also within walking distance of this hostel is San Francisco's REI Store located at 840 Brannan Street,

Tel (415) 934-1938. This superb outdoor store offers a range of backpacking food and fuel, as well as all manner of hiking gear.

Some JMT hikers will nevertheless prefer to travel to Merced and do food shopping in this smaller, more compact town. Merced (pronounced 'Mer–**said**', with the accent on the second syllable), a small city with a population of around 60,000, is dubbed the 'Gateway to Yosemite'. The town was founded in 1889 and today has a fairly lively downtown area of shops, financial institutions and local government buildings, with a large civic centre. There are several supermarkets in town, but probably the best, with a wide variety of choice, are Savemart, on 'G' Street and Olive Avenue, and Albertsons, also on 'G' Street, directly opposite Savemart. There is another

Looking back towards the north-west down to Lake Majorie during the ascent to the Pinchot Pass (Day 16)

Savemart a little closer to the centre of town, on 'R' Street and Main. A good hardware store, from where plastic buckets suitable for posting supplies to Muir Trail Ranch (see 'Posting food on ahead', below) can be bought is Orchard Hardware Stores.

Transport in Merced, as nearly everywhere in the States, is something of a problem. You will need to get from your motel/hotel to a supermarket and possibly hardware store, and then to return to your place of accommodation with your heavy and bulky purchases. This is America – so forget buses! Unfortunately, at least at the time of the author's visit, there are too few taxis for the size of the town; often a very long wait is required, so order your taxi well in advance. Another alternative is to hire a car. This can be done for a minimum period of 24 hours, and costs around $50–$60 for the cheapest type of car. This should be a serious consideration if there are at least two or three people in your party: the convenience of a car will be greatly appreciated.

Remember, that shops and other facilities in Merced, like anywhere else, change with time. It is always best to enquire locally when you arrive.

Posting food on ahead

I know of one group of extremely fit and experienced backpackers who carried all their food for the JMT from the beginning to the end of the Trail. This is exceptional and beyond the

capabilities of most walkers. So most people have to post food on to be stored and retrieved later in the trip.

There are several locations on the first half of the JMT to which food parcels (generally known as 'hiker food caches') can be posted for collection later on during the walk. But from Muir Trail Ranch, roughly at the half-way point of the Trail, there are no further opportunities, so food for the rest of the trek (10 days) has to be carried from Muir Trail Ranch to the end of the walk at Whitney Portal.

The locations to which food may be posted and retrieved later are as follows from north to south, Yosemite to Whitney:

- Tuolumne Meadows: Day 3
- Reds Meadow: Day 7
- Vermilion Valley Resort: Day 9
- Muir Trail Ranch: Day 11.

Which food parcel drops you use requires careful consideration. The best place, by far, to send food packages is Vermilion Valley Resort. It is situated a little before the half-way stage of the hike and charges only a nominal sum to collect and store packages. Furthermore Vermilion caters particularly for JMT and PCT hikers, and you are assured of a warm welcome.

The other three locations all have some disadvantages with food package collection, storage and retrieval. Tuolumne Meadows is only three days from the start of the trek (two if Half Dome is omitted). This means that if a food parcel is posted

View from Silver Pass (Day 9)

from Merced or Yosemite Valley to Tuolumne Meadows Post Office and Store it is likely to arrive after you get there on foot. A way round this would be to take a bus from Yosemite to Tuolumne Meadows the day before you intend to do the hike. Leave your food for the next stage of the walk at Tuolumne Meadows Post Office and Store and return to Yosemite Valley by bus. There are daily buses between the two locations during the summer holiday season. This, of course, is time consuming and results in the loss of a day. Alternatively you may be able to find someone at Yosemite Valley who is driving to Tuolumne Meadows and whom you can trust to deposit your food parcel at the Post Office and Store.

The main problem with Reds Meadow is that the resort charges a fairly high fee (but not nearly as much as Muir Trail Ranch, see below) to collect and store packages for later collection. Also, it is only six days from Tuolumne to Vermilion, so if a food parcel drop has been made at Tuolumne, a drop at Reds Meadow is not necessary. (Alternatively, Reds Meadow could be used rather than Tuolumne Meadows, in which case there would be 6½ days for the parcel to arrive if posted just before the start of the hike).

Muir Trail Ranch is the last place where food parcels can be collected, and even here this means that 10 days' worth of food must be carried. So there is a great need for a food package collection here. The service offered at Muir Trail Ranch is, however, very expensive indeed, and the type of package that must

	FOOD SUPPLY STAGES				
Stage		Days	Distance *(miles)*	Ascent *(feet)*	Descent *(feet)*
1	Yosemite Valley (Happy Isles) to Tuolumne Meadows	3	31.3	8000	3450
2	Tuolumne Meadows to Reds Meadow	3.5	38.8	5500	6300
3	Reds Meadow to Vermilion Valley Resort	2.5	29.7	5300	5200
4	Vermilion Valley Resort to Muir Trail Ranch	2	21.8	4400	4400
5	Muir Trail Ranch to Whitney Portal	10	111.8	23,500	22,700
Totals		21	233.4	46,700	42,050

be sent (plastic bin, see below) adds to the complication and expense. It must be stated, however, that the very high fee charged by Muir Ranch ($50 per in 2010) is probably justified, considering the remoteness of the location and the difficult terrain involved, requiring both the use of boats and pick-up trucks.

The best advice is to use only Vermilion Valley Resort for a food package mail drop. But this tactic is possible only if you are fit enough and have enough space in your backpack to carry nine days' food in the first instance and 12 days' worth for the second stage of the walk. Otherwise, use one or more of the other re-supply points.

The table 'Food Supply Stages' summarises all the points at which food supplies can be posted along the JMT. (Details of the recommendations governing the sending by post of food parcels to the various resorts en route are given below.)

Collection and storage services operate only during the summer hiking season, usually mid-June to mid-September. It would be wise to check the up-to-date requirements for sending, receiving and storing food packages at the resorts immediately before leaving for the US. You can do this by checking out the websites of the resorts (see Appendix 6). Posting of food packages is best done at Merced or San Francisco. Note that Merced Post Office does not open on Saturdays (or Sundays), but one can post items from Mail Boxes, Etc, a 'mailing company', a type of business common in the States. Mail Boxes, Etc is located in Albertson's Plaza in Merced, and is open from Friday to Saturday (Saturday, 10am to 3pm). All materials for packaging your supplies can be bought in Merced or in San Francisco. Make sure you use the appropriate US postal rate when mailing your parcels.

Do not send perishable food through the post, and note that it is illegal to send white spirit or other inflammable fuel through the postal system. (Both Vermilion Valley Resort and Muir Trail Ranch sell white gas, ideal fuel for MSR stoves.) Note that park ranger stations will not accept hiker food caches.

Tuolumne Meadows
Post Office and Stores

A food package can be forwarded to Tuolumne Meadows Post Office, which is situated inside the store there. The post office is generally open only on weekdays, from 8am until 5.30pm. Address the package(s) to 'Your Name', General Delivery, Tuolumne Meadows Station, Yosemite National Park, CA 95389. US postal regulations require the post office to keep the package for a minimum of 10 days.

Finally, note that Tuolumne Meadows, Reds Meadow and Vermilion all have food stores, and so some hikers may elect not to post food ahead to these locations. If you decide on this option, then remember that the choice of food will be much more limited at these stores than at large town and city supermarkets. Also, late in the season, by September, these stores may have reduced their food stocks to very low levels.

Reds Meadow Park
Station and Resort

A package pick-up service operates between 15th June and 10th October. Reds Meadow will pick up packages, not to exceed 14ins high, 14ins wide and 24ins long, at Mammoth Post Office for a charge of $25 per pick-up. They will store it at Reds Meadow

Fisherman at Purple Lake (Day 8)

free for the first five days and then at $1 per package per day thereafter. See www.redsmeadow.com/pdf/PackagePickUp.pdf.

Address the package to 'Your Name', c/o Reds Meadow Resort, PO Box 395, Mammoth Lakes, CA 93546. The staff of Reds Meadow visit Mammoth Post Office about four times a week. Mail the package by US mail first class (parcel post can take up to 30 days to arrive!). Parcel pick-up is at Reds Meadow Store only between 7am and 7pm daily throughout the summer season.

For up-to-date information go to: http://www.mammothweb.com/redsmeadow/form.html.

Vermilion Valley Resort
Use US mail rather than parcel post. Address packages to: 'Your Name', Vermilion Valley Resort, PO Box 258, Lakeshore, CA 93634. There is an $18 handling charge for the first package and $10 for each additional package. Limited to 25lbs per package. Vermilion Valley Resort keeps packages for a maximum of 30 days. The Resort recommends using UPS rather than USPS if less than 14 days is allowed between posting until pickup (but this uses a different address – see www.edisonlake.com/resupply.htm).

For up-to-date information go to: www.edisonlake.com.

Muir Trail Ranch
Food packages should be contained within 5-gallon plastic buckets with snap lid. These can be bought from hardware stores in Merced, and are airtight and mouse tight (there are mice in the food storage shed at Muir Trail Ranch). The maximum weight for each package is 25lbs.

Address the package to: 'Your Name', Muir Trail Ranch, PO Box 176, Lakeshore, CA 93634. Write the date on which you expect to pick up the food supplies on the top of the package. Post as early as possible, two to three weeks before you expect to pick it up, if possible. The charge for collection at Muir Trail Ranch is $45 per container.

For more up-to-date information go to www.muirtrailranch.com/resupply.html or email: howdy@muirtrailranch.com.

It is advisable to send a separate letter to the establishments to which you have posted food packages, informing them that you have sent a package and of the approximate date you intend to collect it.

Angling
Some hikers supplement their diet with trout caught in the lakes and rivers in the wilderness. The fly-fishing is generally extremely good. Note that not only will a small rod be required but also a special permit: enquire at the Wilderness Centre in Yosemite before setting out on your trek. The permits are easy to obtain and inexpensive.

High mountain country near Woods Creek (Day 17)

WALKING THE TRAIL

GENERAL FITNESS AND TRAIL FITNESS

An unfit person attempting the John Muir Trail is not only putting themselves at considerable risk but also, if part of a group, significantly affecting the other members of the party. A general level of fitness is therefore a prerequisite for undertaking the Trail.

But each type of physical activity requires its own type of fitness. Regular day-walkers who take only a light pack each time they venture out will find the burden of a heavy backpack intolerable unless they have carried one on a regular basis for at least a couple of months before the trek. Backpackers who have previously confined their activities to relatively low-level, easy country will find the terrain of the Sierra Nevada exhausting.

The author often leads commercial walking holidays and finds that most people, simply because of the modern working lifestyle, are fit for a day walk provided they then have a week sitting in an office to recover. There may only be minor problems, such as a slight blister or sore knee, at the end of the first day of a walking holiday. If this happened at home then these would have disappeared by the time of the next weekend's walk. But on a walking holiday, the next day-walk takes place the following day...and the next walk the day after that, and so on. These minor problems have no time to heal and soon, usually by mid-week, one or two clients have to take a day off to recover.

Mount Huxley seen from Sapphire Lake, upper Evolution Valley (Day 13)

This is fine on a hotel-based, one-centre holiday, or even on a British or European long-distance-path walking holiday, where each night is spent in a town or village where food and accommodation are available.

But on a hike of the nature of the JMT a day off can only be taken at a few places along the Trail, and none after the mid-way point. Anyone who takes a day off and is not carrying enough food for this extra day out in the wilderness is going to have problems, either of starvation or of a long several-day detour to resupply. So rest days must be planned, not taken at whim.

It is a truism that the only real training for walking is...walking. Similarly the only proper training for backpacking is backpacking. Anyone unused to long walks carrying a heavy load will discover muscles they never thought they had! The best form of training is to go on a walk, preferably in the hills, at least once a fortnight, beginning the year before attempting the JMT. Try to put aside about two or three weekends in the four months preceding your trip to America to go on two- or three-day backpacking trips in the mountains, carrying all your gear. If at all possible try a week-long backpacking trip in the mountains of Britain or Europe about six weeks before your JMT adventure.

Probably, even with all this preparation, you will find the JMT hard going at times, particularly during the first few days and at the beginning of the second half of the trail when setting out with 10 days' worth of food from Muir Trail Ranch. Whatever training you do will not fully prepare you for the heat and altitude of the Californian Sierra Nevada. However, you will almost certainly find yourself becoming trail-fit as the days go on along the JMT: the aches and pains will be less noticeable, the weight of the backpack will become less of a burden, the heat less of a strain, and you may not even notice the altitude.

Whatever you decide to do, make sure that you have some sort of training programme in the months leading up to your JMT trip. It will pay great dividends. But don't think of it as merely 'training'. Rather you are creating possibilities for climbing that Munro that you always wanted to have a go at, for example, or walking that long-distance path you fancied.

HEALTH AND MEDICAL CONSIDERATIONS

Setting out on the JMT in ill health, to trek through an extensive high-altitude wilderness area in the heat of a Californian summer, is asking for trouble. Try to keep as healthy as possible in the weeks leading up to the trek; eat well, avoid overwork and stress as much as possible, and get plenty of rest and sleep. And try to keep away from anyone with a heavy cold or flu! Walkers with long-term medical conditions should first check

with their GP as to the advisability of tackling the trek.

The main difference between walking JMT-type wilderness trails and long-distance paths in Britain and Europe is that hikers on the former have to be much more self-reliant. They are often several days from medical help. Even if there is a doctor or nurse in the party, they will be able to do little without modern medicines and medical equipment.

It is therefore even more important on the Trail than in 'normal' life to do everything possible to avoid medical problems and reduce the risk of accidents. Common sense goes a long way. Concentration, particularly when on rough ground, will reduce the risk of a fall with a heavy pack. This book and other manuals cover such topics as river crossings, encounters with wild animals, and first aid in mountain and wild country situations. But however well read, careful, mentally alert and sensible you are, accidents can always happen, and you must be psychologically prepared to deal with any such occurrence. It is a good idea if at least one of the party has an up-to-date first aid qualification.

JMT hikers should give consideration to general health and medical matters before they go, and in particular the following topics.

Diarrhoea and Stomach Problems

Traveller's diarrhoea is the most common minor illness suffered by those travelling abroad and is due to a sudden change in food, water and climate. Some of the symptoms, but not the cause, can be treated by gut-paralysing agents such as Imodium. Take care to ensure that the stresses of walking the JMT do not allow this mild form of diarrhoea to develop into a more serious condition. If the condition persists then use of rehydration salts (see below) should be considered. Diarrhoea is also caused by drinking contaminated water, resulting in bacterial or protozoan infections (see under 'Water purification' below). Diarrhoea causes a general weakness in the body, and will very significantly affect a walker who is having to cope with the high physical demands of the JMT.

Dehydration

Dehydration can result from excess sweating, diarrhoea and vomiting. Fluid loss will always be considerable in the hot climate of California, particularly at altitude, and it is essential that a sufficient intake of safe water is maintained. If dehydration begins to pass from the mild stage and threatens to become more serious, it is advisable to administer a rehydration solution. Sachets such as Dioralyte are a useful addition to a first aid kit, but without these a simple rehydration solution of 8 level teaspoons of sugar + ½ teaspoon of salt to 1 litre of treated or filtered water can be made up, assuming that you are carrying both sugar and salt! Use of oral rehydration is particularly

important in cases of severe diarrhoea where fluid loss is sudden and considerable. It is better for a fellow member of the party to care for the reydration of the patient, as the victim's own judgement may be impaired.

Sunburn and Heat Exhaustion

Many overseas walkers will be unused to the intense, day-long sunlight of a Californian summer, and those on the JMT have no respite from it. It is very important to wear a sunhat and a high-factor sunscreen, as UV levels at the altitudes of the Sierra Nevada are high and the dangers of skin cancer should not be underestimated. Badly burnt skin also speeds body dehydration. Sunglasses should be worn most of the time.

Carrying heavy loads under the glare of a hot sun at altitude is very stressful on the body, and if sensible precautions are not taken and insufficient fluids consumed then significant medical problems can result. Heat stroke is a very serious condition that can result in death within a few hours if not treated. In a victim of heatstroke, sweating diminishes and body temperature begins to rise. Walking soon becomes staggering, and the patient becoming incoherent, delirious and confused. It is essential to cool the patient as rapidly as possible. The best method is to get the patient into shade, soak the clothed body in water (lie in a shallow stream if possible) and fan to cool the body by evaporation.

High mountain peaks surrounding Evolution Lake (Day 13)

Hypothermia

This is less likely to occur during the usual summer conditions in the Sierra Nevada, but these are high mountains that can have snow and low temperatures at any time of the year. Temperatures at night can drop to very low levels, especially at some of the high camping areas on the second (southern) half of the Trail. Extreme cold coupled with wind and rain or snow are optimum conditions for the development of hypothermia, particularly for the tired and perhaps poorly clad backpacker.

In colder conditions there can be a temptation not to stop to put on warmer or rain- and wind-proof clothing. Resist this temptation if the conditions start deteriorating rapidly. Be sure you are versed in the symptoms of hypothermia and can recognise them in others. Symptoms include slurred speech, lethargy, disorientation, difficulty with co-ordination and irrational behaviour. Get the patient out of the wind, cold and wet. Put up a tent and get the affected hiker into a sleeping bag. Make a hot drink, and ply the patient with plenty of hot, sugary liquids. If not treated the patient can slip into a coma, after which death can result.

Blisters

Even seasoned walkers can develop blisters on the JMT, due principally to the heavy backpack (the body is not used to having to support additional weight on the soles of the feet) and to sweaty feet resulting from the heat. Do all you can to prevent blisters developing – use only well worn-in and familiar boots, and take off boots

69

to remove tiny pieces of grit as soon as you feel them, not after tolerating them for an hour or two. Start your trek with brand new socks and wash frequently. If you are unfortunate enough to have blisters treat them with 'second skin', which should allow you to continue without too much discomfort. If you decide to burst the blister to remove the fluid within, then sterilise the needle first (passing it through a flame immediately before use is the best method) and take great care not to allow the wound to become infected (remember that you are some way from medical assistance).

Athlete's Foot and other Fungal Infections

Hot, sweaty feet exacerbate these problems. If you suffer from athlete's foot be sure to bring some anti-fungal powder on the trek. Untreated fungal infections can become much more serious. 'Crotch rot' is another fungal infection not uncommon in walkers in hot climates. Ringworm is another embarrassing fungal skin infection. Practise good personal hygiene to cut down the risk of such infections.

Dry and Cracking Skin

In the Californian High Sierra during the summertime the air and land are usually very dry and dusty. Dust seems to find its way into every crevice of the body, particularly up the nose. Prolonged exposure to these drying conditions, which are

experienced on the JMT, can lead to a drying out and some cracking of the skin, particularly on the hands. This can be rather painful and unpleasant. Take a small quantity of a moisturising cream with you and apply daily; this may prevent the condition occurring, or will at least ease the symptoms.

WATER PURIFICATION

In any upland wilderness area bacterial contamination of open water sources can occur from time to time, particularly on land used for sheep grazing, or where deer herds roam. In the United States, as elsewhere, water in mountain lakes, streams and rivers may be contaminated with, among other pathogens and parasites, the protozoan known as giardia (*Giardia lambilia*).

Giardia, a single-celled protozoan, is carried in cyst form in the faeces of infected people and animals. Poor backcountry backpacking techniques, particularly poor sanitation near waterways, have led to an increase in giardiasis, a debilitating disease characterised by persistent watery diarrhoea, the expulsion of excess foul-smelling intestinal gas, and muscle and abdominal cramps. Antibiotics are ineffective against the disease, which is usually treated with the drug metronidazole (Flagyl), although this has been shown to be somewhat carcinogenic in laboratory mice and rats and so unnecessary use of this medication should be avoided. If untreated the intestinal surface may be damaged and food absorption impeded, leading to further complications.

It is pretty grim to come down with giardiasis in, say, an Asian city (the author writes from experience!), but at least in such a situation rest is possible and medical attention available. In the Californian wilderness neither luxury is very likely. Even to pack up camp and put on a heavy backpack when feeling so ill is a herculean task, but to then spend several days walking over high mountain passes in such a weak state would test the strength of even the strongest long-distance backpacker. Take every precaution not to contact giardiasis or any other protozoan or bacterial water-borne infection.

Another organism of concern is *Cryptosporidium*, an intestinal parasite found in contaminated water. Symptoms of cryptsporidiosis include a watery, foul-smelling diarrhoea that may persist for up to 10 days. The organism is resistant to chemical water treatment, even the use of iodine. Aquamira is said to be effective against it, but the best way to ensure that water is free of the parasite is to boil it for at least 5 minutes, and ensure that all food is well cooked.

Prevention is far better than cure, and if sensible precautions are taken then all should be well. Be extremely careful with personal hygiene at all times, but especially when close to

popular camping areas and water sources. Despite the advice you may receive from some American trekkers, never drink untreated or unfiltered water from mountain streams or lakes, even if it is fast flowing. It is simply not worth the risk. Spring water is, however, generally quite safe to drink untreated, but be absolutely sure that its source is a natural spring. Two reliable springs are at Muir Trail Ranch (Day 11) and at the Crabtree Ranger Station (Day 19).

There are three methods that can be used to ensure that water is safe to drink: boiling, and chemical and filter treatment.

Boiling Water

This is the most effective purification method and kills nearly all known pathogens. Five minutes of boiling is generally recommended to ensure all microbial life is dead. The disadvantages of this method are that a lot of fuel is used in boiling the large quantities of water required on the JMT, and the water has to be cooled before it can be consumed, a time-wasting process. But untreated water can be used for cooking dehydrated meals as long as the water is boiled for around 5 minutes. Remember that water boils below 100°C at high altitudes, so allow a longer boiling period when in the high camps.

Chemical Treatment

There are three main types of chemical treatment for water: chlorine based, iodine based, and other more sophisticated chemical treatments. Chlorine-based water treatment is not recommended for use along the JMT, as *Giardia* and *Cryptosporidium* are resistant to chlorine treatment; chlorine is mainly effective against bacterial agents.

Iodine is the simplest, cheapest and most reliable chemical to use for water purification in the Sierra Nevada, but its major disadvantage is the foul taste it imparts to the water. This can partly be overcome by adding powder flavourings to the water. Iodine should not be consumed over long periods of time as this can have deleterious medical effects on the body. However, during the short period of the John Muir Trail there should be no or few problems with its use. (There are exceptions, however: neither pregnant women nor people with thyroid problems should consume iodine.)

Iodine can either be used in liquid form or as tablets (iodate), but check the 'use-by date' on the bottle first. Be sure to follow the instructions carefully, particularly with relation to the quantity of iodine required to treat a given volume of water and the time required for the chemical to act (the colder the water, the longer the time required).

Another chemical treatment involves the use of Aquamira. There is no chlorine or iodine in Aquamira, so the treated water is neither discoloured nor foul tasting. This water-

treatment kit consists of two chemicals stored in separate small plastic bottles. When Part A is mixed with Part B in a separate vial for a few minutes the liquid turns yellow as chlorine dioxide is activated and oxygen is released in a highly active form. When added to water, this will kill bacteria, viruses and protozoa, including *Giardia* and *Cryptosporidium*. The treated water is odour and taste free.

The manufacturer states that Aquamira-treated water is safe to drink on a regular basis. The disadvantages are that the process is more expensive than conventional chemical treatments and, like these, the procedure is time consuming. The two parts of the solution must first be mixed together, then there is a wait of a couple of minutes before this mixture can be added to the water, and then a further and longer wait before the water is safe to drink.

Filter Treatment

The disadvantage of all forms of chemical treatment is the time they require. Impatience at this point could lead to the consumption of contaminated water. In addition, the hot climate of summertime California requires large quantities of water to be consumed, and so over a three-week period considerable quantities of chemical are needed for water treatment, and there is always the risk of running out.

Both these problems are avoided by the use of a water filter. Large

The water of Lyell Fork river glides and plunges over wide granite beds (Day 4)

quantities of water can be filtered relatively quickly, and once filtered the water can be consumed immediately. Most American hikers use some sort of water filter when trekking. Although a water filter entails a not inconsiderable initial cost and extra bulk and weight to carry, its benefits on an expedition of this nature far outweigh these disadvantages. One filter is sufficient for use by three or more people, so weight and cost sharing is possible. Remember that the filters should periodically be replaced in the unit as per manufacturer's instructions.

There are two basic types of filter, gravity filters and pump action filters. The latter are to be recommended for giving large quantities of filtered water quickly. It is important to ensure that the pores of the filter exclude all pathogenic bacteria as well as *Giardia* and *Cryptosporidium*. Follow the manufacturer's instructions, particularly with regard to replacing the filter. Most good-quality filters will provide more than enough water to last your JMT hike (at least 160 litres per filter). A greater choice of water filters is available in the US than in Britain, so if time is available make your purchase in the States.

Note for 2010 Reprint: a survey has found that only about half of the hikers on the JMT are treating their water prior to consumption, the rest imbibing freely from stream and lake water. Do so if you wish, but in the author's opinion it is not worth the risk.

COPING WITH ALTITUDE

Moderately high altitudes are reached on the JMT. The Trail is mainly above 9000ft (2750m); three passes are above 10,000ft (3048m), three above 11,000ft (3351m), two above 12,000ft (3658m) and two above 13,000ft (3962m), with Mount Whitney reaching 14, 496ft (4418m). Acute Mountain Sickness (AMS) can occur at these altitudes and trekkers should be able to recognise the systems.

The itinerary for the JMT suggested in this guidebook should allow for altitude acclimatisation. Starting the hike at the Yosemite, or lower, end of the trail allows for gradual acclimatisation, the walker slowly becoming used to the lower oxygen concentrations in the air at higher elevations. As the hiker proceeds south the passes slowly increase in altitude, and the trek culminates at the highest point of all on the summit of Mount Whitney.

Mild altitude sickness is perhaps at times to be expected. The major symptoms are headache and sluggishness, but the headache should respond to mild painkillers.

Two potentially fatal consequences of altitude are high-altitude pulmonary oedema (HAPE), characterised by breathlessness, fluid on the lungs and a hacking dry cough, and high-altitude cerebral oedema (HACE), in which fluid builds up in the brain. The only cure for both HAPE and HACE is to descend. If descent is delayed these conditions are likely to become fatal. Further information on the risks, avoidance and treatment of altitude sickness, HAPE and HACE can be obtained from publications/websites on mountaineering medicine.

Most people are not significantly affected by altitudes below 8000ft. However, some individuals seem to be more prone to altitude sickness than others, and at lower altitudes. Although the heights reached on the JMT are only moderate, they are sufficient in unacclimatised people to result in altitude sickness. Common sense and gradual acclimatisation are usually all that is required to ensure safe passage at the altitudes encountered on the JMT.

DEALING WITH BEARS

Unless you are experienced in walking in bear country, the subject of bears is unlikely to be far from your mind – the likelihood of seeing a bear, what to do in the event of an encounter, how to protect your food from the animals and so on. However, in all probability, providing you follow some sensible rules, you will never set eyes on one of these huge mammals during your whole sojourn along the John Muir Trail. When the author walked the JMT the group encountered a bear on only one occasion, when at night an inquisitive animal wandered into our camp looking for food. But we had stowed food

TIPS FOR WALKING IN BEAR COUNTRY

If you follow these tips you are likely to enjoy a safe and bear-free trek.

- Always be alert for the presence of bears. Evidence of their passing will be obvious to the alert backpacker: bear stools are often seen on the Trail and their freshness will indicate when the animal passed that way. Often long, deep claw marks will be seen on tree trunks beside the Trail. You need to be lucky and have some experience to pick up bear prints along the path.

- If at all possible hike with a group of people rather than alone. Bears will be much less likely to cause trouble if they are heavily outnumbered.

- Don't go quietly in the woods. Talking together, singing, whistling, etc, all serve to let bears know that you are about, and they will then probably keep out of your way. (Note that this doesn't mean making a terrific amount of noise when in the wilderness; do respect the tranquillity of the landscape and do all things in moderation).

- Most bad encounters with bears have occurred when the bear has been surprised and then rushes at the victim in panic. If a bear comes into your camp at night make a lot of noise, bang pots and pans together, etc, and it is then quite likely to take fright and retreat.

- Don't walk at dusk or just after dawn, when bears are likely to be active, particularly near streams and other water sources, where they may go to drink at this time of day.

- If you do come across a bear stop immediately. Do not approach or make any sudden moment; if you run they may give chase, and you will have no hope of outrunning them. Slowly back away, keeping an eye on the animal at all times.

- The worst scenario is to encounter a female bear with its cub. It is essential in such a case never to pose a threat to the cub or to get in between the mother and its offspring.

correctly and after a short while and a lot of noise (created by us not the bear!) the animal left without harming either us or our equipment.

Probably the best small book on the subject of how to cope with the presence of bears is *Bear Aware, Hiking and Camping in Bear Country* by Bill Schneider (see Appendix 7 – Bibliography). It is an American publication, but acquire a copy if you can and follow the simple advice it contains. If you do so the chances of an unhappy encounter with a bear are remote. Don't let the fear of bears ruin your trip.

The first thing to note is that there are no Grizzly Bears in California. These were wiped out by the white settlers during the nineteenth century. So you only have to contend with the Californian Black Bear (*Ursus americanus*), which tends to have dark brown fur rather than black. They are smaller than the massive grizzlies and less aggressive, but nevertheless they are large and dangerous wild animals and must be treated with respect. In fact more humans have been hurt by Black Bears than by Grizzly Bears.

It is useful to have a few facts about the biology and lifestyle of the Black Bear. They weigh between 150 and 500lbs and are up to 8ft high when standing. Bears are omnivores, eating almost anything, but are opportunists, preferring to go for the easiest attainable food. They can run at over 30 miles an hour, so never think that you could outrun a bear. They can easily climb trees. Bears are more active around dusk and at dawn, but can remain so throughout the day, particularly if the weather is cool. They rarely venture above the tree line because little food is to be found there, so you are not likely to encounter a bear above about 9000 or 10,000ft. Their most acute sense is that of smell, which is many, many times greater than that of man.

A park ranger told the following anecdote which neatly sums up the

senses of the larger animals in the parks of the western US: 'A leaf fell in the woods. The eagle saw it, the deer heard it, but the bear smelled it!'

Most of the trouble with bears over the years has been attributed to humans feeding them. Once fed they will quite naturally come again and make a nuisance of themselves. If they do so persistently the rangers may decide to transfer them to another, less popular part of the park, or in exceptional cases, when an animal becomes a real danger to the public, they have to be shot. The stupidity of man is nearly always the cause of one of these magnificent beasts being shot.

A few American backpackers carry a bear-repellent 'pepper spray' for use if attacked by a bear. Firstly, it should be noted that these are not available in the UK and can be bought only in the US. It is illegal to import one into the UK. Secondly, most rangers and seasoned backpackers are of the opinion that such a device is unnecessary on the JMT, and few people along the Trail appear to carry one. If the precautions outlined in this guidebook are practised, it is very unlikely that you will have a bad bear encounter.

Finally it should be noted that some areas along the JMT are more renowned for bear problems than others. The worst areas are said to be in the Yosemite Valley and Little Yosemite Valley, in Lyell Canyon between Tuolumne Meadows and the Donohue Pass, and at the

TIPS FOR COOKING AND CAMPING IN BEAR COUNTRY

Following these tips while camping and cooking will significantly reduce the risk factor from bears.

- Store food in bear barrels or boxes (see below).

- Avoid strong-smelling foods and try to cook well before dusk so that the smells of cooking have dispersed before darkness falls, the time when bears are likely to be most active.

- Keep your cooking area some distance from your tent/sleeping area, and keep all food and cooking smells out of the tent.

- Wash off immediately any food that is spilt on your body or clothes, and never retire to your tent at night without doing this.

- Do not store food or toiletries in your tent, and never, never sleep with such items in your tent.

southern end of the Trail particularly after the Kings river and in the Mount Whitney area. The Onion Valley region (off route of the JMT) is also notoriously bad for bears. However, more high-risk areas could develop in the future as bears become wiser and more persistent, and if troublesome bears are moved by park rangers out of one area and into another. Always check the current situation with a knowledgeable park ranger on your arrival.

Note for 2006 Reprint: Although in the past areas above around 10,000ft in the High Sierras have been bear-free, there were some reports in 2005 that bears had been seen up to 12,000ft in the vicinity of the JMT. One backpacker in that season had his barrel snatched and mistreated by a bear at the last lake before Glen Pass (Day 17).

Note that the use of bear barrels is obligatory along most of the JMT.

Protecting food from bears

For bears in modern-day California humans mean only one thing: food. If they trouble you it will almost certainly be because they are after the food you are carrying. The golden rule to remember, above all others, is that if a bear does manage to get hold of your food then never, never try to get it back. The bear will defend his prize vigorously and you will almost certainly be hurt.

Many of the bears now found in the backcountry areas were originally located in the developed areas of the parks such as Yosemite Valley. Here they learnt to raid rubbish bins and break into cars after food and so were relocated to the wilder parts of the park. But by then they had learnt the skills of stealing food from humans and so continue to be a nuisance.

Try not to leave backpacks unattended and never walk away from bags containing food. Unattended food will quickly be found by bears. It has already been noted that bears have a very acute sense of smell. A ranger once told the author that a bear can smell the coke *inside* the can 50 yards away! Whether or not you consider this to be an exaggeration it does indicate how strong a sense of smell these animals have.

The traditional method of protecting food supplies during the night was to hang them from the branch of a tree out of reach of bears. Several backpacking manuals outline this technique, and so it will not be repeated in detail here. Suffice to say that food must be hung from a tree branch high enough to prevent a standing bear from reaching it (around 12ft is recommended), and far enough from the trunk (around 10ft) and below the branch (at least 5ft is recommended) to make it difficult for bears to reach. It's not easy, believe me!

However, as bears have increasingly come into contact with humans in wild-country areas, so they have learnt various tricks to retrieve food hung from trees. As one ranger told the author: 'It will take you half an hour or more messing about trying to hang your food, but it will only take the bear a minute or two to get it down!' The more times bears are

successful at retrieving such food the more times they will try again. For this reason the technique of hanging food from tree branches is actively discouraged in many areas, and is even prohibited in some, such as the Mount Whitney region.

Bear barrels and boxes are now the recommended method of food storage in bear country (see below), and it is likely that the practice of hanging food will be banned in an increasing number of areas. Be sure to determine the current regulations with regard to the hanging of food when you begin your trip. If you do intend to hang food, don't forget that you will need a long length of cord, but never do so in areas where the technique is illegal.

Bear Barrels

The preferred method of storing and carrying food is now the 'bear barrel' or 'bear canister'. The use of bear barrels is likely to increase in the future and may become the only permitted way of carrying food into national parks and wilderness areas.

A bear barrel is a cylindrical container that a bear cannot hold easily or open. There is an sealable lid on the top of the bear barrel, which is fastened by a flush thread that is easily opened or closed using a coin or a screwdriver (Swiss army knives should have one of these tools). A bear is thus prevented from opening the canister. The barrels are also strong, and cannot be damaged even by bears sitting on them, pounding them or throwing them, so the food remains safely inside. Bear barrels also conveniently double as campsite seats, useful when preparing food or sitting around a campfire.

Bear barrels do solve the problem of protecting your food from bears quite effectively. However, this does come at a price. The major disadvantage is that bear barrels are heavy, bulky containers. Made of thick, heavy plastic and metal in the case of the cheapest barrels, most weigh at least 2.5–3lbs when empty. They are also bulky, and somehow have to be fitted either inside or onto the outside of your backpack. The standard barrel measures around 12–15ins in length and has a diameter of about 8 or 9ins. Hence the volume for storing food inside the barrel is not great, and it will hold no more than four to five days' food for one person. This is a problem on the longest stage of the JMT, from Muir Trail Ranch to Mount Whitney, when up to 10 days' worth of food must be carried. However, larger and lighter bear canisters are coming onto the market, made from titanium and other lightweight but very strong materials. These barrels will probably be capable of carrying up to 10 days' worth of food.

For a small fee bear barrels can be hired from the National Park Ranger Office (in the Wilderness Center, which is about 50 yards from the Visitor Center) in Yosemite Valley and used for the duration of the hike to Whitney Portal. A credit card will be required for this, as a hefty deposit must be paid. If you do not return the barrels then this charge will be made to your credit card. When you arrive at Lone Pine at the end of the JMT, post the barrels back to the Yosemite Valley rangers' office. This is a routine procedure – there should have no problems doing this at Lone Pine Post Office.

Bear barrel with dehydrated food

Evolution Lake is passed en route to Muir Pass (Day 13)

Bear-barrel hire is a popular service with overseas backpackers. Thus, during the high summer season, you may find that all the barrels have been hired out, and have to wait a day or two for them to be returned. To avoid this, phone the park rangers' office in Yosemite as soon as you arrive in the US and ask to reserve your barrels – if you can guarantee the day and time of your arrival.

The alternative to hiring is to buy your own bear barrel, and more and more seasoned American backpackers are doing just that. The advantages are obvious: you can obtain a large but light canister (ones for hire tend to be relatively small and heavy); there is no risk of finding that the park office has hired out all the barrels; and there is no need to post the barrel back to Yosemite – you can take it home and use it on a later trip.

But bear barrels, particularly the large, light titanium ones, do not come cheap! You could delay your decision until you get to Yosemite Valley, where the barrels are usually on sale in the shops. If you want more information on bear barrels, then try entering 'bear barrels' on a good web-search engine. It should come up with all the information you need. Try for example searching for 'bearikade – Wild Ideas' on the web. The SIBBG (Sierra Inter-Agency Black Bear Group) website is also a useful one. It is the official site for approved bear-proof food canisters in Sierra Nevada, and provides details of all approved bear storage, with links to the suppliers' sites (see Appendix 6).

Bear Boxes

Another solution to the problem of storing food safely away from bears is the 'food storage box' or 'bear box'. Some of the camping areas along the Trail have these large metal food-storage containers, which are bear proof provided that the door is shut tight. If they were found at regular intervals along the Trail then they would solve the food/bear problem at a stroke. However, they were not common in many of the areas along the JMT when the author did the trek. Where they do occur they should be used for storing all foodstuffs and scented toiletries, toothpaste, cosmetics and the like. The location of bear boxes along the JMT at the time of writing is given in Appendix 4, but visitors should check out up-to-date information.

The long-term policies of the various park and forestry authorities along the Trail with respect to the use of bear boxes are unclear. The

trekker should ascertain the current situation when he or she arrives in Yosemite.

RIVER CROSSINGS

Never underestimate the potential danger of crossing rivers on the Trail. Fatal accidents do occur. By making the trek in August and crossing rivers in the morning wherever possible (before the sun has melted any high-lying snow) the trekker will probably experience few problems with river crossings on the JMT, unless it is an exceptionally wet summer or there was a heavy snowfall very late in the spring. But remember that conditions vary considerably from season to season, and from week to week. It is quite possible to experience high rivers and swift currents with dangerous crossings in early July. Consider yourself

Twilight at Lone Pine Lake campsite above Whitney Portal (Day 21)

Camping for the night at Deer Creek Campsite (Day 7)

fortunate if you hike during a long dry spell, when river levels should be low.

JMT hikers should acquaint themselves with the basic techniques for crossing rivers. A trekking pole is often useful, helping to stabilise the walker. If necessary link arms with other trekkers to form a stable group. Learn to judge the speed and strength of river currents. Remember also that swollen rivers often go down quite rapidly in a few hours, so if in doubt always wait until conditions improve. If in doubt, it is always preferable to wait for other hikers to arrive at the scene to form a larger, more stable group for a difficult crossing. Finally, never be afraid to retreat altogether and find another way out of the wilderness by one of the escape routes (see Appendix 3). It is far better not to complete the JMT than to die in the attempt!

OTHER NATURAL HAZARDS

In addition to those covered above, there are a number of other natural hazards that you may encounter.

Forest Fires

In the tinder-dry conditions of a Californian summer forest fires are not uncommon in the natural forests of the High Sierras. The cause of forest fires is often a lightning strike, but humans – either by accident or malicious intent – are sometimes responsible. Large fires can be devastating. Take all sensible precautions, particularly when lighting fires and using stoves, so as not to be the cause of such a catastrophe. When on the Trail be aware of any fires that are burning in the region, and if at all concerned try to contact a park ranger, several of whom are on duty during the summer months, for information and advice.

Thunderstorms

Thunderstorms are potentially life threatening, because of the real possibility of lightning strike, particularly on Mount Whitney and on Half Dome, the latter being a particularly dangerous place in such storm conditions because of the metal cables. Hikers should be particularly vigilant and avoid the most dangerous areas and positions when a storm is imminent. A typical daily weather pattern starts at around 10am, with small clouds developing as those seen in the photograph on page 161, which by early afternoon often form into stratus clouds, overcast and greyer (see photograph on page 166). These usually clear by the evening. After a few days of this pattern, the air gradually becoming 'heavier', thunderstorms may develop by late afternoon.

If this weather pattern appears to be establishing itself, it would be wise to time high exposed passes for the mornings, not during the afternoons. If you are hiking late in the season, the first big storm of winter, possible in late September, will probably be known about for many days beforehand and news of this should be available from Rangers, and from hikers on shorter walks.

Mountain Lions

Pumas (cougars) live in the Sierra Nevada, but they are shy, mainly nocturnal mammals, so encounters with humans are rare. It is extremely unlikely that you will see one of these big cats, but if you do chance upon one then there is really only one thing to remember: don't run! It may be very hard to resist this basic instinct, but a fleeing person is reacting just like the animal's prey, and could trigger an attack. If this happens there is no way that you could possibly out-run the animal. Make no sudden movements, but slowly back off, and the chances are that the puma will lose interest and walk away.

Marmots

This rodent is somewhat smaller than the Alpine Marmot of Europe. Marmots have sharp teeth and will chew at anything to get at food. This includes your expensive high-tech tent and your backpack, if left unattended. There always seems to be a resident marmot on duty at the Muir Hut on Muir Pass (Day 13). In particular, care should be exercised when leaving packs to climb Half Dome (Day 1) and Mount Whitney (Day 20). At lower altitudes, chipmunks and squirrels can be a nuisance to hikers.

Mosquitoes

The number of mosquitoes on the trail varies considerably from year to year and from week to week, although as a general rule there are likely to be more of these irritating biting insects early in the season than in mid to late summer. Unusually heavy and late snowfall, and a wetter July than average, often result in mosquitoes and flies being unseasonably rife and unpleasantly abundant later than is normal. Some JMT hikers, the author included, were hardly bothered at all by 'mossies', while others have reported that in some areas the situation has been almost intolerable. Be sure to take plenty of insect repellent (see First Aid Kit Box, page 52), and a mosquito/ midge hood has been strongly recommended by some readers of this guidebook. The good news is that Californian mosquitoes do not carry serious diseases such as malaria.

Hornets

These stinging insects can be extremely aggressive and when swarming can be a serious threat. If badly stung, medical treatment will be required. Take every precaution not to disturb a hornet's nest. Keep an ear, as always, to the Trail grapevine and take special care if passing through an area where hornets have been seen by others. The author witnessed a bad hornet attack on a child who had unwisely disturbed a nest of the insects. It was a most unpleasant sight.

Snakes

Poisonous snakes are common throughout the West and you may see a snake occasionally. Most snakes are shy animals that avoid contact with humans. As long as care and common sense are used they pose little threat. Be alert, never approach or try to touch a snake, give one a wide berth if seen, and never step over a

fallen log without looking to see if a snake may be curled up on the opposite side.

LOW-IMPACT TREKKING AND NATIONAL PARK/ WILDERNESS REGULATIONS

The national park authorities do a marvellous job in conserving the wilderness environment through which the JMT passes. This landscape is very fragile, and thoughtless action by trekkers and campers would quickly lead to deterioration. Help to keep this land in its pristine state by practising minimum-impact trekking. All camping areas should be left so that there is no evidence of your passing. You should also be aware that there are a number of regulations (outlined below) that apply in national park and wilderness areas. Failure to comply could result in a very steep fine.

A key element of minimum-impact camping is the 'pack-it-in and pack-it-out' principle. This means that paper and other combustible materials can be burnt on a campfire, but non-combustible items such as aluminium liners (often used in packaging of dehydrated foods) must be carried out. Similarly, no non-biodegradable rubbish should be buried, it all must be carried out.

Official regulations limit the use of campfires above certain heights, but these vary for different areas. At the time of writing this height was 9600ft for Yosemite National Park,

10,000ft for Kings Canyon National Park and the John Muir and Ansel Adams wilderness areas, and 11,200ft in Sequoia National Park. These regulations are applied to preserve the environment. Many of the trees are thousands of years old and some are sub-fossilised. There is insufficient tree growth for the trees to replenish themselves. The various authorities may alter their height restrictions in the future, so be sure to check the current regulations before setting out on the Trail.

The disposal of human waste requires important consideration. There are very few toilets along the trail, but where they are found – use them. For the most part it will be necessary to 'go wild', and a lightweight plastic trowel is highly recommended for burying waste. These are available from good camping/backpacking stores. One per 3–4 people in a party should be sufficient. Bury waste and used toilet paper in a hole at least 8ins deep (if buried in shallower holes it is easy for wild animals to dig up). The official line nowadays is that toilet paper should neither be buried nor burned, but packed out instead. In wilderness areas it is prohibited to deposit body wastes within 100ft of streams, lakes and trails. Refer to the excellent book explicitly entitled *How to Shit in the Woods* (see Appendix 7 – Bibliography).

Do not wash yourself or your clothes with soap or non-degradable detergents when in the wilderness;

Human-waste bin at Whitney Portal

use only biodegradable detergents for this purpose. These can be bought in good camping/backpacking gear shops. Washing and/or discharging soap wastes (including biodegradable soap – even this pollutes) within 100ft of lakes or streams is prohibited within wilderness areas.

The following activities are also prohibited in national park and wilderness areas:

- shortcutting a switchback (zig-zag)
- entering without a permit
- processing or storing food or refuse in a manner that allows bears to access it
- discharging a firearm.

CAMP ROUTINE

Those who have until now walked long-distance trails by staying in bed and breakfast establishments, hotels, gîtes or alpine huts will find the experience of wilderness camping initially quite challenging. Even those who have camped frequently in official campsites in Britain and elsewhere, transporting all their camping gear and food by car, will find that wilderness camping requires greater effort and planning. However the benefits are also measurably greater. There is nothing that compares with a night under the stars, far away from the trappings of the modern world; and nights spent 'under canvas' in wilderness California will remain fond memories in the years to come.

Wilderness camping involves a lot of work – there are more tasks to accomplish than when staying at an organised camp site. Apart from the obvious tasks such as selecting a relatively level and comfortable area on which to pitch your tent, and then erecting it and sorting out sleeping and cooking gear, there are other time-consuming jobs to do.

There is no convenient tap from which to draw water; it must be collected, so hopefully you have not camped too far from its source! Then it must be treated, either chemically or by filtration, another job that will probably take longer than anticipated. Water used for drinking and cooking has to be treated (see 'Water

purification', above), although when the cooking process involves boiling water for several minutes this will normally kill harmful organisms. Large quantities of water are required for keeping your body hydrated and for cooking dehydrated food. Additionally, water that will be needed during the day has to be treated in camp before leaving in the morning. After cooking, food containers and cutlery have to be washed and rubbish sorted, packed or burnt.

It is a good idea in a party of three or more to organise a division of labour. It will usually become obvious which members of the group are good at specific tasks, and who detests certain jobs; work out an amicable division of labour amongst yourselves and make sure that the tasks nobody likes doing are shared out equally among the whole group.

There will be several hours between the group stopping for the evening and the tired camper crawling into his or her tent. Relaxation time in the evenings is very important on a trek of this nature, and so it is important to complete essential tasks quickly and efficiently in order to allow plenty of time for rest, reflection and relaxation. Disorganisation in the campsite means that routine jobs take an inordinate amount of time, thus leaving hikers little time for 'switching off', mentally and physically, and recovering from the exertions of the day. Members of the group thus retire late in a far from relaxed mood, a poor preparation for the following day on the trail. Similarly, inefficient breakfast preparation and camp breaking can cause a late start, which may lead to the main climb of the day being undertaking in the fierce heat of a Californian midday, rather than in the relative cool of early morning. You should aim to have breakfast and break camp within 1½hrs of rising.

Establishing a camp routine during the evening stop and morning preparation will help to make light work of the many tasks that are a necessary part of camp life on the trail. It will no doubt take a few days to establish a workable system, but from then on life in camp should run smoothly and allow plenty of spare time to relax and savour the wilderness.

TIME DIFFERENCE

California is in the Pacific Time zone, which is GMT minus 8hrs. American Daylight Saving operates between the first Sunday in April and the last Sunday in October, during which time the clocks move forward 1hr, so California will then be on GMT minus 7hrs. However, during the same season the UK is on British Summer Time, which is 1hr ahead of GMT. California is therefore 8hrs behind Britain during the summer months.

Be sure to allow for the effects of jet lag when planning your trip to the States to walk the JMT.

PUBLIC HOLIDAYS IN THE US

The only public holidays in the US likely to concern the JMT hiker are Independence Day (4th July) and Labor Day (the first Monday in September). On public holidays banks, schools, government offices and post offices are closed and public transport is limited to a Sunday schedule. It is wise to be aware of these festivals if they fall either on the few pre-JMT days or the post-JMT days of your trip. But in the wilderness these days will pass like any other day.

MONEY

Plastic cards are the main form of currency in the US. It is extremely useful to carry a credit card, particularly if you intend hiring a car before or after undertaking the JMT, and/or if you expect to go on a shopping spree before returning home. ATMs (automated teller machines) are found almost everywhere in the States, and certainly in San Francisco, Merced, Lone Pine and Los Angeles, where your usual bankcard should enable you to withdraw cash from these machines. Traveller's cheques in US dollars are another safe and convenient way of carrying funds. Remember that except for pre- and post-JMT days, and at some of the backcountry resorts situated along the northern half of the Trail, you will have no opportunity to spend money! Even the smallest stores, for example at Reds Meadow and Muir Trail Ranch, accept plastic, so the only cash you really need is a ten cents piece for opening the bear barrel! Vermilion Resort operates a 'tab' system whereby payment for all services and goods is made, by credit card or cash, at the end of your stay.

INSURANCE

Failure to hold medical insurance while in the US could be the biggest mistake that you ever make. Medical treatment in the US is extremely expensive; couple this with a mountain rescue from a wilderness area, and the uninsured person may live to regret that he or she survived!

Make sure that sufficient cover for medical expenses is included in any policy, and that mountain rescue, including the use of a rescue helicopter, is fully covered. Make it very clear to the insurance company what you will be doing during your stay, and insist that an accompanying letter is sent with your policy declaring that your activities on the JMT are fully covered.

Some Alpine Club members are automatically insured for mountain activities, but be sure to check whether the sum insured is sufficient. British Mountaineering Club members (or affiliated clubs) can insure through the BMC. You would be advised to also take out general travel insurance, because such Alpine Club policies usually cover only mountain activities, so you won't be insured

88

while, for example, walking down the street in San Francisco or in Merced. Snowcard (www.snowcard.co.uk) is a well-priced insurance tailored to adventure sports, whose mountain insurance covers general travel (such as lost baggage), illness, accidents and helicopter rescue.

THE NATURAL WORLD
by Dr Charles Aitchison

GEOLOGY OF THE SIERRA NEVADA

The Sierra Nevada is, by geological time scales, a young mountain range, still changing and growing. Its geologic genesis rests on aeons of cataclysmic events within the earth's crust.

Five hundred million years ago the region was at the bottom of a Palaeozoic ocean, and for 300 million years silt from coastal streams and fine fall-out from countless volcanoes settled in layers miles thick. About 200 million years ago powerful forces within the crust folded and compressed the compacted silt strata, causing chemical changes and hardening. Other forces broke the strata and crushed enormous pieces together, sliding some beneath others until very slowly they reared up against one another and mountains began to emerge.

During those times masses of molten granite, from far within the Earth, forced their way towards the surface.

Hexagonal and pentagonal basalt blocks of the 'pavement' area of the top of the Devil's Postpile (Day 7)

Molten rock burst through in weak areas to build volcanoes, but most cooled and hardened below ground as huge granite bubbles, the bedrock of today's Sierra Nevada. By about 80 million years ago the granite had coalesced into an underground floor. Meanwhile the whole mass was rising slowly, with broken layers of stone from the formerly submarine strata lying on top of the granite bedrock. Streams cut through those overlying hills, wearing down the landscape as rapidly as it rose. Water ate away the old rock until the granite domes and ridges emerged.

Between 30 and 5 million years ago further volcanic eruptions covered the streams and valleys and all but the tallest peaks under thousands of feet of steaming mud. Towards the end of that period the entire Sierra began to bow up in a west–east arch, and west winds brought rain and snow to the steepening slopes, creating new rivers.

The arch gradually began to fracture, and enormous blocks worked loose and fell. This went on for 10 million years, while quantities of volcanic material spilled from fissures east of present day Mammoth Mountain, so much so that the landmass collapsed inward, forming the Long Valley. Some time between 3 and 10 million years ago, the apex of the arch rose above 14,000ft, the present elevation of the Sierra crest. The most severe ruptures happened within the last 700,000 years. The crest line of the range is still rising slowly, and an earthquake in 1872 raised Mount Whitney by several feet. The Owens Valley floor shakes to about 20 earthquakes annually.

Over the last 2–3 million years an entirely different force – glaciation

– has finished the work of mountain-making by chiselling, carving, polishing and gouging out some of the deepest valleys in America. John Muir wrote 'Nature chose for a tool not the earthquake but the tender snowflowers, noiselessly falling through unnumbered centuries'. Generations of glaciers came and went at least six times, beginning 2–3 million years ago, and formed today's Sierra Nevada. The present Sierra ice fields are not leftovers from prehistory but the younger remnants of a cold cycle called the Little Ice Age that occurred as recently as the 15th–19th centuries.

VEGETATION AND FLOWERS

Over 1500 flowering plants, shrubs and trees are found within Yosemite National Park, and there are many more to add to the total as the John Muir Trail winds across three more national parks, two wilderness areas and down the drier eastern slope towards the Great Basin. The Sierra Nevada is wonderful, wild, fragile and savagely beautiful, and its landscape, animals and plants are still being changed by elemental forces of wind, water, fire, ice and falling snow.

This section on the vegetation of the Sierra Nevada and of the flowers along the John Muir Trail is intended to enhance hikers' knowledge of, and pleasure in, their environment by describing the intimate relationships between the many region's beautiful

flowers and awesome trees and its climate and mountains. Yosemite and Tuolumne Meadows Visitor Centers and The Store at Whitney Portal sell informative leaflets, guides and books on the area's plants.

Life Zones and Their Vegetation

Between the highest point of the Sierra Nevada at Mount Whitney (14,497ft) and the lowest, near the El Portal entrance to Yosemite National Park (2000ft), there is a huge climatic and vegetation range, which biologists have divided into five life zones, each with characteristic vegetation. In Yosemite Valley spring starts in early March, but it reaches the sub-alpine and summit peaks only in August.

Foothills zone: This is the warm, western slopes of grassland, shrub and open woodland up to about 5000ft. After cool, wet winters spring brings colourful wildflowers, which disappear again to become dormant during the hot summers.

Mixed conifer zone: Here summers are less warm, with summer showers. This forest grows between the foothills and the Red Fir/Lodgepole pine forests higher up the mountains. The zone extends from 3000ft to 6000ft in the north of the region to 5000–8000ft in the southern Sierra.

Twenty-five of the 43 Californian conifer species grow in the Sierra. They are dominant in the vegetation, with a powerful presence, tall and of great girth. There is a mix of towering trees, Ponderosa or Yellow pine, Sugar Pine, Jeffrey Pine, Douglas fir, White Fir, Incense-Cedar and the Giant Sequoia. The latter forms groves at altitudes to 6800ft.

Colourful under-storey shrubs grow in the mixed conifer forest, including the red-flowered Sierra Gooseberry, with spiny berries; the Thimbleberry, a white-flowered, large-leaved raspberry; the prominent Green-leaf Manzanita, with its inverted urn-shaped flowers; and Deerbrush, covered with fluffy panicles of white flowers in June/July.

Red Fir/Lodgepole Pine zone: This forest covers a large area. Depending on latitude, it grows at heights between 6500ft and 8500ft. Growth is controlled by a cool climate and short growing season. The area is under 8–20ft of snow for 8 months of the year, and most plants flower quickly after snowmelt before the dry summers. Summer days can be warm with afternoon thunderstorms, but night temperatures can fall below freezing.

Red Fir grows on slopes of deep rocky soils, while Lodgepole Pine grows along edges of wet meadows and well-drained areas. It also fills large areas to the timberline. Scattered through the zone are Western White Pine and Jeffrey Pine. White Fir grows on the zone's lower slopes, and Mountain Hemlock reaches the timberline.

The forest under-storey is mostly a mix of wild gooseberries and red currants, with low plants of the heather family: Pine Mat Manzanita, a sprawling, pale green-leaved plant; White Heather, a creeping plant with round bells on upright shoots; Mountain Heather, with bells of purplish pink. In moist areas are found Alpine or Californian Laurel, with clusters of open pink bells, and Labrador-Tea, with clustered heads of white flowers; occasionally, even at this elevation, Western Azalea scents sunny clearings with its yellow-blotched, white flowers. The berry-bearing bushes are a delight to the Black Bears, and in season the bears' fresh droppings of fruit pips and skins indicate their presence, even if they are not seen.

Subalpine and arctic-alpine zones: This zone is extensive in the Sierra. The timberline reaches nearly 7000ft in elevation in the north, and almost 11,000ft in the south. Conifers of the subalpine forest are Whitebark Pine, Lodgepole Pine, Mountain Hemlock, Western Juniper and towards the south Foxtail Pine. Lodgepole pines grow as weathered shrubs around the timberline.

Above the timberline is the alpine zone, with open expanses of moist and dry meadows, screes and rock. There are glaciers, and snow lies deeply for much of the year. The growing season is a short two months with summer thunderstorms. Summer days are rarely very warm, and frost and snow can occur on any day.

Flowers Along the Trail

This section follows the trail from Happy Isles, Yosemite Valley, at an altitude of 4035ft. The next lowest point between the start and Mount Whitney is 7400ft, near Reds Meadow. Most of the trail is at elevations in the Red Fir and Lodgepole Pine forest and above. Many flowers recur at intervals in particular habitats. The trail is usually walked from June through September, so the flowers en route will vary with the season.

Many backpackers start walking the trail on a hearty breakfast at Curry Village. The walk to Happy Isles through wooded meadows along the Merced river passes bushes of white-flowered, red-berried Mountain Dogwood; the Mountain Violet, with yellow-faced and purple-backed petals; Western Azalea, here flowering in June; and on the gravel flats tiny pink flowers packed tightly into soft heads of Pussypaws, which despite its delicate appearance grows up to the timberline.

In wet, rocky places, on the climb approaching Nevada Falls, the delightful Red Columbine and the White-flowered Bog Orchid grow. The columbine's nectar attracts humming birds. Up on Half Dome an evergreen bush, Chinquapin, with spiny-covered edible nuts, fills the granite crevices. Approaching Sunrise Creek the dusty trail is lined by low, silver-leaved Brewer's Lupines. The brilliant Sulphur Flower grows on the sunny rocky flats approaching Sunrise camp.

On the campsite's moist, grassy clearing, the large meadow and streamside the blue Sierra Gentian and the Alpine Gentian are frequent. The latter, growing to over 10,000ft elevation, displays stemless white flowers externally striped in purplish dark brown. Mingled with them is the little yellow Meadow Monkey Flower and magenta Lemmon's Paintbrush.

At 8600ft, just under the treeline, Tuolumne Meadows' large expanse is filled in July and August with thousands of flowers, among them the low Shooting Star in bold magenta-pink, Northern Gentian, the white Ladies' Tresses Orchid, and along the Lyell river the large Lupine and rosy-headed Swamp Onion. Tulip-like white Mariposa Lilies grow in stony places on the ascent from Lyell Canyon. Scarlet Gilia, another humming-bird flower, is conspicuous in sunny forest clearings around Soda Springs and Reds Meadow.

On high, north slopes the conifers give way in places to scrub birch and shrubs: *Jamesia americana*, a plant with no local name and clusters of pale pink flowers; Cream Bush, bearing rows of closely packed pinky-white tiny flowers; Mountain Spirea's stems topped with flat masses of rose-purple flowers; Shrubby Cinquefoil, with yellow rose-like flowers; Tobacco Bush with its white flowers; and the Red Elderberry.

Subalpine moist meadows suit the Explorer's Gentian, erect stems with 1–3 funnel-shaped flowers of dark blue, striped green; and the bright yellow Alpine Monkey Flower. Many subalpine and alpine herbaceous plants grow as low mats or tight tuffets and many are silvery haired These forms give protection from the elements, ferocious cold in winter and desiccating winds and intense sunlight in summer. High, bare slopes grow silver-leaved, yellow-flowered, scarlet-seeded Oval-Leaved Buckwheat, and the fleshy-leaved, white-flowered Alpine Saxifrage fills the spaces between boulders. The rocky trail is lined by flaming orange California Fuschia, lavender Mountain Pennyroyal, a red Paintbrush, rosy-red Newberry's Penstemon, Rock-Fringe with its leafy mats of rose flowers, and yellow Wallflower.

Above 10,000ft, from the west of Mather Pass, the boulder screes are laced with ribbons of the Sierra Primrose. In company with them, at the highest altitudes, from Forester Pass and to the summit of Mount Whitney, is the Sky Pilot, its flowers in shades of blue. Mixing with the blue on Mount Whitney is a glorious golden daisy, the Alpine Gold.

BIRDS OF THE JOHN MUIR TRAIL

As the John Muir Trail winds up and down along the Sierra Nevada, backpackers walk daily through varied terrain and habitats of differing vegetation zones. Each day, therefore, many different kinds of birds can be seen, but walking with head down and a heavy backpack does not make for ideal bird watching. When you stop for breath, a rest, a snack, or at camp look up at the sky and the trees, for you may spot any of a number of species.

Books and checklists of birds are available at the visitor centres and shops at Yosemite and Whitney Portal. Yosemite's list gives 154 species that may be seen along the way, and Whitney Portal's has 241. Long lists are difficult to use en route, but one of the Peterson Field Guides, *California and Pacific Northwest Forests*, is compact and illustrates and lists birds by different habitats. Knowing which birds are most likely at any place makes identification easier. A summary of birds commonly seen in particular habitats is given below (although a number of species frequent more than one habitat).

Birds of open areas: The trailhead campsites and areas around outdoor eating places often have groups of Brewer's Blackbirds running around. Towards dusk the flocks join into larger groups flying towards their roosting sites. Flights are dramatic silhouetted against sunset. Large birds such as Common Ravens, Golden Eagles, Red-tailed Hawks and Turkey Vultures are easily spotted calling and wheeling at times to great heights.

Birds of the forest: Steller's Jays are noisy black-and-blue birds with large crests. They approach close,

93

attracted by food scraps around camp grounds. Blue grouse, about the size of a domestic fowl, inhabit forests to all levels, as does the Mountain Chickadee, a tit with a greyish back, a black cap and throat. White-crowned Sparrows are recognisable from the many other birds that look like sparrows by their pink bills and conspicuous black-and-white striped heads. Two black-and-white wood-peckers, the Hairy Woodpecker and Williamson's Sapsucker, the latter distinguished by its yellow belly and red throat, forage round tree trunks. Other woodpecker species frequent forests at different levels, and in places, such as Reds Meadow, the dead wood left after forest fires provides excellent nesting sites as well as wood-burrowing insects for food.

Rivers, lakes and adjacent forest: Several specialised birds frequent this habitat, but many of the forest birds may be found here too. Deciduous trees such as California Sycamores, alders, ash, poplars and willows grow along the riverbanks. A rich under-storey of berry-bearing shrubs grows with them and provides cover for colourful Belted Kingfishers as they perch quietly on branches overlooking water. In flight they give a loud rattling chatter. The diversion across Lake Edison to Vermilion resort by the ferry is an opportunity to sit back and watch ospreys fishing. The rare California Gulls, which nest by a few high mountain lakes, disperse after

breeding and stop over at larger lower lakes en route to the coast.

Mid-elevation pine forest: This is a zone of mixed conifers, with Ponderosa and Jeffrey's pine dominant. The diverse mix of tree species and under-storey shrubs provides habitats rich in bird species, especially warblers and owls. Seven species of owls nest within Yosemite National Park, and if not seen by day may be heard at night. The Great Horned-Owl is the largest American owl by weight and is easily recognised by its ear tufts. The Great Grey Owl is the largest by length and is found in forest trees at all levels. The various warblers flit about searching twigs for small insects. The Brown Creeper, a small, solitary bird, creeps up tree trunks, often in a spiral fashion, searching for insects. Another tree specialist is the Red Crossbill, which moves about in flocks searching for conifer cones. The birds can hang upside down while they open cones to remove the seeds. Pygmy and Red-breasted Nuthatches, like tiny woodpeckers, can go head-first down trunks in their insect searches. Two colourful members of the thrush family, the American Robin and the Western Bluebird, feed on the ground hunting for worms and insects in the leaf litter. Cooper's and Sharp-shinned hawks hide among branches to dash out suddenly to catch unwary birds.

Montane fir forest: Here White Fir, Red Fir (often in pure stands), Lodgepole Pine, Western White Pine and Mountain Hemlock are the dominant conifers. Conifer seeds are the main food of a number of colourful forest finches: Cassin's, Evening Grosbeak and Pine Grosbeak. Clark's Nutcrackers are noisy birds of the crow family, with grey bodies and white patches on black wings and tails. They move around in family groups searching for seeds. It may seem strange to look for hummingbirds high in the mountains, but two species, the Calliope Hummingbird and the Rufous Hummingbird, are migrants and feed and nest up into the subalpine zone. They are attracted to red flowers, and their sounds may first bring them to your attention.

Subalpine forest: This scenery is wildly spectacular. Open timberline groups of gnarled, long-lived, red-barked Western Juniper, Foxtail and other pine species edge wildflower meadows. Here Lodgepole Pines grow as weathered shrubs at timberline. Elemental granite outcrops and screes contrast with colourful flowers. Even in summer the weather can be severe, and nights can be very cold. The Great Grey Owl commonly hunts in the subalpine meadows. The meadows in Yosemite National Park are good places to look for it. American Dippers hunt the streams under water, as they swim and walk over gravel beds looking for insects and tiny

fish. Migrant species of insect-eating flycatchers, sparrows, thrushes and warblers find the brief summer long enough to rear their broods. The male Mountain Bluebird is another conspicuous member of the thrush family, though it lacks the rusty-red of the Western Bluebird.

Alpine tundra: There are no trees above the timberline, but many kinds of birds common at lower levels can make this their summer home. A few kinds breed only in this region. Grey-crowned Rosy Finches range as high as the summit area of Mount Whitney and approach close to people if crumbs are offered. They nest under boulders in scree and in rock crevices. Water Pipits, tawny birds with thin bills, sing from high overhead. When hunting the grassy edges of lakes and mountain streams for insects their tails are constantly bobbing. The White-tailed Ptarmigan of the screes are more likely to be heard than seen. Their plumage changes with the seasons, becoming white in winter, and feathers grow on their feet to ease walking over snow. Their cackling calls are part of the magic of the mountains.

MAMMALS ALONG THE TRAIL

The Sierra national parks, national forests and wilderness areas set aside permanently by the Wilderness Act of 1964 encompass country ranging from little above sea level on the east to

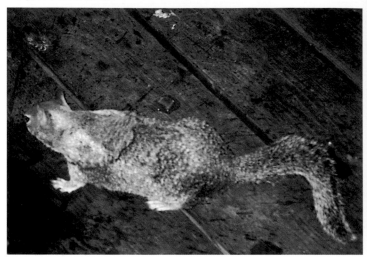

Californian Ground Squirrel

Golden-mantled Ground Squirrel

the high summit of Mount Whitney. The terrain varies, with lakes, rivers, marshes, grasslands, forests, alpine vegetation above timber line, screes, bare rock, cliffs and glacial ice. Periodically parts are swept by hurricanes, avalanches and lightning fires. Despite the summer heat and the harsh winter snow and cold the Sierra is home to a number of specially adapted animals. The John Muir Trail gives access to this special place where many of these animals may be seen. The commonest are squirrels of various sorts, raccoons, deer and bears. The last of these, if not seen, may be heard at night by campers around the tent!

Yosemite Valley animals are accustomed to people and are relatively tame. Coyotes will at times sit in the road to stop cars in the hope of being fed and can look most put out if not given anything! They are smaller and more lightly built than wolves and usually live alone or in pairs. Their normal food is small mammals, but they will eat carrion, fruit, tubers and even plants when very hungry. Their calls may be heard at night.

Western Grey Squirrels are common, inquisitive animals, which may scamper around campers' feet, under the outdoor picnic tables, collecting crumbs to take away to store for later. Their unmottled and unspotted upper parts distinguish them from the Californian Ground Squirrels, which have brown upper parts, flecked whitish or buff. The latter are common on dry ground. When dusk approaches Raccoons wake up and forage. They are found in the Sierra Nevada woodlands, near streams, lakes or ponds. They rest by day in trees. They get much food from the water, eating mainly fish, crayfish and frogs, but are omnivores eating any small animals in addition to fruit, nuts, green plants and picnic remains dropped or thrown in trash bins. Winter is spent in semi-dormancy.

After leaving the valley, on the diversionary route up Half Dome, you are likely to see Alpine Chipmunks. These animals are found only in the Sierra Nevada and can be seen to 12,500ft on Mount Whitney. Chipmunks resemble small squirrels but have striped faces. They nest underground and climb trees. The eight Sierran species look much alike but don't mix, with each occupying a specific habitat and altitude. Yellow Pine Chipmunks live in open coniferous forest at mid-elevations on western slopes and are brightly coloured and distinctly striped. The dark brown, less conspicuously striped, Townsend Chipmunks are larger and live in deep forest; they are as often found in trees as on the ground. The Lodgepole Pine Chipmunk is the commonest, inhabiting all high-elevation closed conifer forest on west and east slopes. The small Sagebrush Chipmunk lives only on the eastern slopes of the Sierra where sagebrush grows, and it can be seen at levels below Whitney Portal.

Yellowbellied Marmot

Chipmunks are found along most of the trail and are fun to watch as they chase each other about on the ground and up and down tree trunks. Cheeky and inquisitive little animals, they can be a nuisance; if they smell food their sharp teeth will quickly chew through any rucksacks left lying around. The presence of chipmunks and other rodents makes it essential that all advance food parcels posted to Muir Trail Ranch are in heavy duty plastic tubs.

Tuolumne Meadows and other high grassy areas are home to another squirrel, the rare Belding's Ground Squirrel. Colonies of this sandy brown animal live in burrows. When approached they sit upright to watch passing tourists and dive headfirst underground if they feel threatened. They are active only from May to

October and hibernate through winter. Another squirrel, which hibernates for six months, is the Golden-mantled Ground Squirrel and is the only striped squirrel. This one is particularly tame around Trail Camp below the eastern cliffs of Mount Whitney.

Marmots are large ground squirrels that live underground and are active during the day. The Yellowbellied Marmots live at alpine levels in areas of boulders where their whistles become a familiar sound along the trail. As they are protected animals they have become used to walkers and beg for food, even becoming a bit of a nuisance to those who stop for a snack on some of the high passes. They do not store food but eat large amounts of green plants to accumulate fat to nourish them through their hibernation.

THE NATURAL WORLD – MAMMALS ALONG THE TRAIL

Other animals along the trail are shyer. You are most likely to see them when you rest quietly en route or at morning and evening camp. Lightweight binoculars are useful. Because hunting is prohibited in the national parks and wilderness areas of the Sierra, Mule Deer, with large ears, are seen frequently in woods and grasslands along the trail and around camp sites. They will approach, feeding slowly as they go through a camp. The deer migrate seasonally to fresh feeding grounds.

The other hooved animal of the Sierra, the Bighorn Sheep, is a shy animal and is not likely to be seen on the trail itself. When the trail is in mountainous terrain, if you scan the high slopes you may be lucky and see these magnificent creatures. Living on craggy slopes of high mountains, often above the timber line, the Californian bighorns are adapted to snow conditions. They are primarily grazers and descend in spring to feed on buds of spruce and aspen and other shoots. During the colder months they feed on berries, lichens and bark, using their hooves to dig in snow. The sexes live in separate flocks.

Woods and grasslands anywhere along the trail are home to many small animals. The species of White-footed and Deer Mice are considered the most attractive of the new world mice. Their colours vary from grey, through fawn to reddish or gold, but all have snow-white underparts and feet.

Several species of Pack or Wood Rats are abundant in deserts and mountains. They have hairy tails and white underparts. They build huge mounds of sticks and litter to nest in. Some mice are insect eaters, while several species of Grasshopper Mice feed almost exclusively on grasshoppers and other insects. Their high-pitched squeaks can be heard 350ft away.

You may also see hares and rabbits. Hares are larger than rabbits and have longer legs and ears. They are solitary, do not burrow and they try to outrun pursuers, whereas shorter-legged rabbits run to refuge in vegetation or burrows. Young hares are born fully furred and open eyed. The Varying or Snowshoe Hare grows a white coat in winter and ascends to high altitudes. The White-tailed Jack Rabbit, despite its name, is a lanky hare, which can been seen at over 14,000ft on Mount Whitney and can survive winter by eating bark. New World Rabbits or Cottontails don't dig burrows but may occupy burrows of other animals. Their young are born almost naked with closed eyes. Brush Rabbits' young are covered in hair at birth. They too ascend as high as 14,000ft.

In any of the forest areas Porcupines, which are large rodents, may be seen walking on the ground, but are more often seen up in the trees, where they feed mainly on bark and buds. Another forest animal, the Sewellel or Mountain Beaver, is not often seen, but its presence can be detected from evidence of the extensive tunnels it digs. It stores food underground for winter. This sole species in its family is not a beaver and is about the size of a rabbit, thickset and short-legged with a tiny tail hidden in its fur. It is found only in north-west California and south-west British Columbia, living in damp areas of dense forests and thickets to 7000ft.

The increasingly rare Pika inhabits the Arctic-alpine zone above the timberline. Pikas are adapted to the snowline of remote mountains and die if the summer temperature becomes too high. They are the size of guinea pigs, with short tails and hairy feet for running across rocks. They make hay, which they dry in the sun before storing it under rocks for winter food. Their whistling calls from scree slopes reveal their presence.

The small animals are preyed on by numerous small, aggressive and fearless predators, such as martens, foxes, badgers, skunks and their kin. The American Marten and the Fisher are rare members of the weasel family. Martens have powerful claws for climbing and bushy tails for balancing. They are even more nimble than squirrels, their common prey. Although arboreal they also hunt on the ground and eat nuts and berries. They remain active through the winter. The Fisher is the largest (growing to 3ft) and the least arboreal of the American martens. It turns porcupines onto their backs to kill them

and can kill deer immobilised in snow drifts. American Mink are solitary and nocturnal animals, equally at home in water or on land and adept at swimming and climbing. They eat fish, frogs, reptiles, small mammals, birds and their eggs. The Red Fox hunts alone, mainly at night, relying on its sensitive nose and ears rather than eyesight. The American Badger is a bulky animal, which swims and climbs efficiently and burrows rapidly to escape danger or hunt for small animals and young birds. Another predator is the Striped Skunk. This well-known animal hunts small animals along the forest edge.

The American Black Bears are the largest predators of the JMT, but they eat a wide range of food – from mammals they catch to fish, grubs, fruit, leaves and carrion. They are not always black; colours vary from pale shades of brown to black. Excepting mothers with cubs, Black Bears are usually solitary and more diurnal than the Brown (Grisly) Bear, which has not been seen in California since 1924. Black Bears spend the winter not in true hibernation but in a dormant state. Bears can be encountered anywhere on the trail, and if not seen they may be heard padding around the tents after dark! They probably cause the most anxiety along the trail, not because hikers fear attack but because bears can scent food at a great distance and are adept at stealing any that is not in a standard bear barrel.

Mule Deer grazing

Two shy members of the cat family, the Bobcat and the Mountain Lion (Cougar, Puma), may occasionally be seen on the trail. All cats have short, powerful jaws and long canine teeth for holding and puncturing their prey. Prey is caught by careful stalking before a sudden close-range rush, killing with a deep bite into the neck or back of the head. The Bobcat is a species of lynx, slightly smaller than the Northern Lynx. Though mainly nocturnal Bobcats may be seen in the day, favouring bushy country with rocky outcrops. Their main prey are Jack Rabbits, Cottontails and small rodents. The Mountain Lion is the largest member of the cat family in the Americas. Males can be 6ft long (excluding the tail) and weigh 225 pounds. In 1963, the year in which the bounty for killing one of these splendid creatures was repealed (12,461 having been killed since 1907), it was estimated that 150 remained in the Sierra. Mountain Lions' chief prey are deer, which are usually hunted at night.

Half Dome from the Merced river in Yosemite Valley (Day 1)

TRAIL GUIDE

Yosemite Valley

The Trail begins in Yosemite Valley: it may be touristy but don't rush through, as there is much to see and some wonderful viewpoints. A one-way road makes an 8.5 mile loop around the valley, serving campsites, viewpoints, the valley 'villages' and various path drop-off points. There are two main 'villages', Yosemite Village and Curry Village. A free shuttle bus operates around Yosemite Valley and is very useful for travelling between the Backpackers' Campsite, Yosemite Village, Curry Village and Happy Isles for the start of the trek.

There are three sights not to miss when in Yosemite Valley.

Yosemite Falls: An easy path leads to the base of these waterfalls. There are Upper and Lower falls, and their combined drop is 2425ft, making this the tallest waterfall in North America.

El Capitan: Take the shuttle bus to Valley View Turnout. From this point there is a good view of El Capitan, the world's largest granite monolith at 3593ft. At night scan the face for torchlight from climbers bivouacking on the high wall.

Glacier Point: This can be reached by bus or on foot if you have the time and energy. It is worth making the effort as it is an excellent view-point, beloved of John Muir. It is over 3200ft above the valley floor and is reached either via Glacier Point Road, off Highway 41, or on foot by steep waymarked footpaths.

Yosemite Village is the main centre of the area, with a visitor centre, muse-ums, gift and other shops, a post office, ranger station and wilderness cen-tre. Your wilderness permits must be picked up from the wilderness centre, which is situated about 50 yards from the visitor centre.

Both Yosemite Village and Curry Village have gear shops, where fuel and most other items of hiking and backpacking equipment can be pur-chased before the start of the trek. There is also a village store in Yosemite Village.

There are several restaurants serving various cuisines in both Yosemite Village and in Curry Village. Restaurants open at 7am for breakfast. It is a good idea to have a hearty American breakfast before setting off on your first day's walk, but beware, as full American breakfasts really are large! Unfortunately, if you do take such a breakfast you will not be able to make the early start that is recommended: Yosemite is at a relatively low altitude, and during a good summer the temperature rises steeply after the early morning cool.

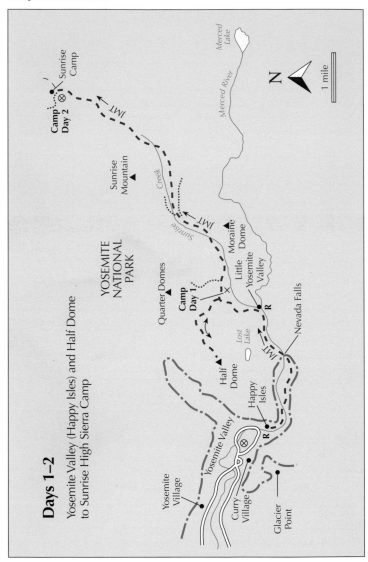

Days 1–2

Yosemite Valley (Happy Isles) and Half Dome
to Sunrise High Sierra Camp

DAY 1

*Yosemite Valley (Happy Isles) to Half Dome Trail
Junction/Sunrise Creek and the Ascent of Half Dome*

Total distance of stage:	12.3 miles
Cumulative distance from Yosemite:	12.3 miles
Total ascent for stage:	5000ft
Total descent for stage:	1850ft
Cumulative ascent from Yosemite:	5000ft
Cumulative descent from Yosemite:	1850ft

Location	Height (ft)	Distance (miles)	
		Sectional	Cumulative
Happy Isles Yosemite Valley	4040	0	0
Vernal Falls	4800	1.6	1.6
Nevada Falls	6120	1.5	3.1
Little Yosemite Valley Campground	6150	1.0	4.1
JMT/Half Dome Trail Junction	7050	2.3	6.4
Summit of Half Dome	8836	2.7	9.1
JMT/I lalf Dome Trail Junction	7050	2.7	11.8
Camping area east of JMT/ Half Dome Junction	7160	0.5	12.3

Map: Harrison Map Sheet 13

The first day on the Trail is one of the best of the whole
trip, not because of the John Muir Trail itself, but for the
ascent of Yosemite's most famous mountain, the spectacular Half Dome. The climb to the summit does not form
part of the JMT, but it would be a great pity for any lover
of the high mountains to walk on past without experiencing the exhilaration of the sensational but aided climb
and enjoying the stupendous views of Yosemite from
its summit. From Yosemite Valley the peak looks out of

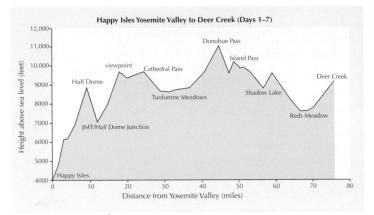

bounds to the ordinary mountain walker, but this trail goes 'round the back' of the mountain, from where an ascent is more realistic for the non-climber. The climb to the top of Half Dome is not for the faint-hearted, and those who cannot cope with a fair degree of exposure should not be tempted to try for the summit.

The ascent of Half Dome will be enough for one day for most walkers, and so a camp is suggested only a little distance after the JMT/Half Dome trail junction. Those not attempting Half Dome should be able to reach Tuolumne Meadows from Yosemite Valley in two days, as indeed could fit and experienced long-distance hikers who include Half Dome. However, to rush through the outstanding landscape of the Yosemite National Park is to miss the point of the JMT. Moreover, this is only the very beginning of your epic journey through the High Sierras, so trail fitness will not yet have been achieved, and the wise will wish to avoid over-exertion at this stage.

The map given at the Wilderness Centre when collecting your permit is not a great help in finding your way around the area, and some hikers have difficulty in locating the backpacker's campground. To get there take the free bus to stop 16, then walk through the North Pines

Campground, following the campground road to the very north of the campground until a sign to the Backpacker's Campground and 'Valley Loop Trail' is located. Cross a small bridge to the delightful and quiet campground that rarely fills. The fee is $5.00 per person (2010).

From the backpackers' camping area in Yosemite Valley Campsite (note that only in an emergency is more than one night allowed at this campsite), or wherever you spent the night in Yosemite, walk or take the bus to **Happy Isles**. Buses start at 7am. To walk to Happy Isles from the Backpacker's Campground, trace your steps back through North Pines Campground to the main road. Cross the road and follow the path alongside the river (this will come out at the trailhead and saves walking down the road – approximately a 30 minute walk).

From the bus stop cross the bridge and follow the signpost for the Mist trail. Soon reach some floodgates on the right and continue on the path climbing to the left, marked to Half Dome and the Vernal Falls. Within 100yds or so reach a comprehensive signboard which shows the distances to various points, including 211 miles to Mount Whitney on the JMT. The good path

North Dome seen from Yosemite Valley

climbs steadily. After about a mile cross a wooden bridge over a boulder-strewn river with a waterfall (the Vernal Falls) above to the left. On the far side of the bridge is a water fountain, the last safe water until Whitney Portal it is said (although this is not strictly true, as good water is to be found in Tuolumne Meadows and at Vermilion resort and a few other places). There are toilets here.

About 5mins later there is a trail junction: ahead is the Mist trail but the JMT climbs to the right, signposted to Tuolumne Meadows 26.8 miles. After another couple of minutes ignore the trail down to the right (for stock only) and follow the path ahead signposted to Nevada Falls 2.5 miles and Merced Lake 12.4 miles. Keep to this popular and well-constructed path as it zig-zags slowly upwards along the side of the canyon wall. Eventually the plunge and water slide of the **Nevada Falls** comes into view, and several giant granite peaks produce numerous photo opportunities. Continue on the path to Nevada Falls. Cross the wooden footbridge over the top of the falls and continue to a toilet block on the left of the Trail. Continue on the Trail for about another mile to **Little Yosemite Valley Camping Ground**. This is the first area since leaving Yosemite Valley that one is allowed to camp. If you wish to call it a day here then bear to the right for about another 10mins or so to the backpackers' campground. Merced Lake is also reached by going to the right at this junction. But for the JMT, bear to the left following the signpost to Half Dome.

Pass the path signposted to the rangers station and continue to climb until you come to the JMT/Half Dome Trail Junction. Here a most important decision will have to be taken: whether to take the side-trail to climb Half Dome, or to omit it and continue along the JMT. Your decision will be influenced by such factors as the time at which you reach this junction, the fitness of your party, the amount of food that you are carrying, the weather conditions and the ability of the party to cope with the extremely steep granite slopes of Half Dome. Allow 2½–3hrs minimum for the round trip from this trail junction to the summit of Half Dome and return, or more if you want to spend some time on the summit admiring this fantastic viewpoint. Do not attempt the climb to Half Dome if there are dark clouds building, and it is afternoon, as fatal lightning strikes are not uncommon on the peak.

JMT hikers will no doubt wish to leave their heavy sacs at this junction whilst attempting the climb. However, there are two important considerations here. Leave food only if it is in bear barrels, or else your backpack is in danger of being severely damaged by bears and your food lost; in addition you will risk a fine from the rangers for feeding these animals. Secondly, take your valuables with you. There are many day-trippers in this popular area, and stolen gear could be heading out of the park by car within a couple of hours of this point; alas you are not in true wilderness yet!

Steel cables protect the route up the final granite pyramid of Half Dome

The **ascent of Half Dome** needs little description. Easy walking on a good path through trees leads to some easy scrambling over rocks, which in turn leads to the base of the summit peak. The climb from here is extremely steep over smooth, polished rock. However, the ascent is aided by a fixed cableway. A pile of thick gloves will be found at the foot of the climb. Do not attempt the climb without the use of these gloves, as not only will your hands be blistered by the cable, but a fall would be difficult to halt with bare hands. Climb between the two cables. Your arms will no doubt ache for days afterwards from all the exertions of pulling upwards on the cables. Those suffering from a fear of heights should not attempt the climb. The fixed cables are erected at the start of the summer hiking season and taken down usually in early October. Do not attempt the climb if the cables are not in place. The Half-Dome cable system was completely renovated in 2005-6. During the main summer season overcrowding on the cables can be quite severe, with waits reported in some exceptional cases of up to ¾ hour just to get onto the cables. Note that between autumn 2006 and summer 2007 three deaths were reported from falling off the Half-Dome cables, although this is atypical, there being no fatalities in most years. You are recommended to start out on the ascent of Half-Dome as early in the day as possible to avoid day-hiker crowds and late afternoon thunderstorms (so leave at first light from the valley if possible).

The option is to continue on to the water, which is from a stream that crosses the Trail. However, this is not a recommended place for camping as bears often frequent this area, particularly at dusk when they tend to make for the stream for water and, no doubt, to check out the food of any backpackers who have been rash enough to camp there.

After climbing Half Dome (or not, as the case may be) pick up your full pack once again and continue along the JMT. After about 5mins or so there are some possible places to camp about 50yds off the trail to the right. Although this spot is not ideal, because water is another 5mins or so (about ¼ mile) further along the trail, it is the recommended place to spend the night. ◀

There is a wonderful view from this **campsite** back to Half Dome, climbed earlier this afternoon, and it is thus a fitting spot to end a great day, your first along the JMT. The two or three 5-minute journeys for water are, after the toil of the day, no real further hardship.

DAY 2

Half Dome Trail Junction/
Sunrise Creek to Sunrise High Sierra Camp

Total distance of stage:	7.6 miles
Cumulative distance from Yosemite:	19.9 miles
Total ascent for stage:	2600ft
Total descent for stage:	400ft
Cumulative ascent from Yosemite:	7600ft
Cumulative descent from Yosemite:	2250ft

Location	Height (ft)	Distance (miles)	
		Sectional	Cumulative
Camping area east of JMT/ Half Dome Junction	7160	0	0
JMT/Merced Lake Trail Junction	7940	2.3	2.3
Viewpoint (top of ascent)	9700	3.3	5.6
Sunrise High Sierra Camp	9360	2.0	7.6

Map: Harrison Map Sheet 13

A short day, in fact the shortest on the whole of the JMT apart from the very last day after Whitney. This will give your body time to recover from the exertions of yesterday's Half Dome climb and to savour this truly remarkable area. There is one fairly steep climb though, so all is not relaxation.

From the **camping area** continue along the trail to reach the stream which you have been using as a source of water for your overnight camp. Immediately after crossing the stream turn right to climb on the John Muir Trail following the line of Sunrise Creek. Follow the path until you reach a trail junction: straight on leads to Merced Lake, but for the JMT turn left, signposted to Tuolumne Meadows (15.6 miles). Within less than ¼ mile the junction with

HIGH SIERRA CAMPS

The stage terminates at Sunrise High Sierra Camp. Sunrise Camp caters mainly for fee-paying guests who stay in hut-style accommodation while on walking holidays in the Yosemite area. The camp usually has a limited quantity of tinned and dehydrated food for sale, but it is best not to rely on this. They may also provide you with dinner and breakfast for a fee, but it is important to note that they are often full up with guests and so have no extra food available. If you would like to stay in their accommodation and eat the meals then you would be advised to book with the camp (tel. 559-252-4848) before you leave Yosemite Valley (or even earlier if possible). There are five or six of these 'camps' in the Yosemite area, all owned by the High Sierra Camps organisation: clients go on short walking holidays in the park and link these camps for nightly accommodation. You may well feel envious of these hikers, as they are unburdened with the heavy pack that you are no doubt beginning to loath – despair not, as your sac will probably seem more manageable as the days progress.

the Forsyth Trail is encountered. This heads off to the left signposted to Tenaya Lake in 7.8 miles. Ignore this path and continue ahead on the JMT, which is coincident with the Sunrise Trail from this point: trail markings here give Cathedral Lake as 9.5 miles and Tuolumne Meadows as 14.7 miles.

Continue along the well-defined path, eventually drawing near to the stream on the left, Sunrise Creek again. After crossing this creek you begin a major ascent. The climbing path is a good one, zig-zagging through the pine trees and granite boulders. After what may seem like an eternity the gradient eases as the trail reaches a high point. A much needed rest here provides a stunning view to the north of Cathedral Peak and Pass. It is just over a mile from here easily downhill to Long Meadows, where there is a dramatic change in the scenery. Amble along the flat plain to reach the campsite up among the rocks on the left. This is the backpackers' area of **Sunrise Camp**. Here there are bear boxes, a water tap (but better to treat or filter the water before drinking) and toilets.

DAY 3

*Sunrise High Sierra Camp
via Cathedral Pass to Tuolumne Meadows*

Total distance of stage:	11.4 miles
Cumulative distance from Yosemite:	31.3 miles
Total ascent for stage:	400ft
Total descent for stage:	1200ft
Cumulative ascent from Yosemite:	8000ft
Cumulative descent from Yosemite:	3450ft

Location	Height (ft)	Sectional	Cumulative
			Distance (miles)
Sunrise High Sierra Camp	9360	0	0
Cathedral Pass	9,700	4.5	4.5
Tuolumne Meadows Visitor Centre	8640	4.6	9.1
Tuolumne Meadows Campsite	8620	2.3	11.4

Maps: Harrison Map Sheets 13 and 12

A relatively easy climb after leaving Sunrise Camp leads to a dramatic viewpoint from where many of the outstanding mountains of Yosemite are on view: Cathedral Peak, Columbia Finger, Tressider Peak and Echo Peak. Cathedral Pass and Cathedral Lakes are a highlight as the Trail begins a long descent to Tuolumne Meadows. Here there is an interesting visitor centre, a large campsite, a post office/store and a café which serves fast food including substantial breakfasts. Tuolumne Meadows, although only three days or fewer by foot from Yosemite Valley, is situated on a main road, with bus connections during the summer months back to Yosemite. A rest day could be taken here as you will probably be quite tired, hungry and dehydrated after the first three days on the trail, and ready food availability means that your precious food supplies will not be consumed while at Tuolumne.

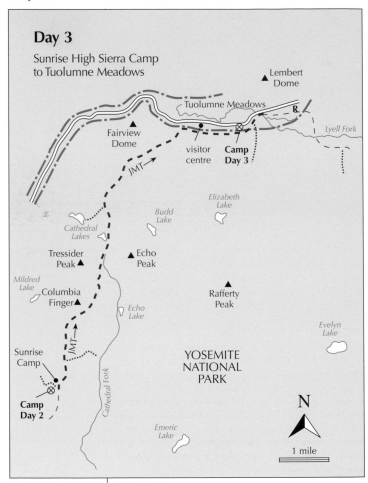

Day 3

Sunrise High Sierra Camp to Tuolumne Meadows

Lembert Dome

Tuolumne Meadows

R.

Fairview Dome

Lyell Fork

visitor centre

JMT→

Camp Day 3

Elizabeth Lake

Budd Lake

Cathedral Lakes

Tressider Peak ▲

▲ Echo Peak

Mildred Lake

Columbia Finger ▲

Echo Lake

Rafferty Peak

Evelyn Lake

Sunrise Camp

JMT→

Cathedral Fork

YOSEMITE NATIONAL PARK

Camp Day 2

N

Emeric Lake

1 mile

Many hikers will have posted food packages on to Tuolumne Meadows for collection at the post office/ store. If your food parcels have not yet arrived then you may have an enforced rest day or two! However, as only three days of walking have so far been undertaken, with

Cathedral Peak above Cathedral Lake

18 still to go, most walkers will perhaps omit a rest day here, but instead have one at Reds Meadow in a few days' time. Note also that officially one is not supposed to spend more than one night at the backpackers' campsite in Tuolumne Meadows.

After a night at **Sunrise Camp** continue on the path around Long Meadows, at the end of which head north on the trail, beginning a steady climb. This is the only significant climb of the day, so bear with it. The reward at the top of the ascent is a magnificent viewpoint of the high mountains of southern Yosemite. **Columbia Finger** is the sharp finger of rock to the south-west, and **Tressider Peak** lies to the north-west. Cathedral Peak is to the north-north-east and **Echo Peak** to the north-east. Do not be tempted to move ahead too quickly: linger to enjoy this stupendous view.

Descend from here on the JMT through Cathedral Pass , noting the large feldspar crystals in the granite strewn over the pass. The initial descent leads to a gorgeous blue lake, Upper Cathedral Lake, situated at 9585ft above sea level, beneath the 10,911ft Cathedral Peak. The descent continues from here, the path soon entering pine woodland again

115

to reach a trail junction. Here to the left is a path signposted to Cathedral Lake (Lower Cathedral Lake), a detour worth taking if you have plenty of time and energy available (but note that bears have been reported to be active at Cathedral Lakes). It is about ½ mile away, with a drop of about 300ft. The JMT ignores this branch path, continuing ahead on the descent: it is 5.5 miles from this point to Tuolumne Meadows, your destination for the day.

After the Cathedral Lake branch point the Trail soon climbs again, but only for a short while, before the descent is resumed. As the descent becomes steeper there are a few unmarked side-paths: ignore these and keep to the main Trail. Descend to a major path junction, a little before reaching the main highway. There should be a map on a board here indicating the trails in Yosemite. Turn right at this point to cross a bridge and follow the direction to Tuolumne Meadows and its visitor centre indicated by a signpost. The path rather surprisingly and disappointingly climbs a little at first. Follow it until you reach a path T-junction. Turn left here to reach the **Tuolumne Meadows Visitor Center** – or right to follow the signposts to the campground. To reach the backpacker's campground the best way is to go to the Tuolumne Meadows store. Behind the store (on the left when facing the store) there is a 200yd cut-through trail to the main campground. On reaching the main campground road turn left and within 100yards the backpacker's campground is signed uphill to the right.

OPTIONAL REST DAY

Tuolumne Meadows

Tuolumne (pronounced 'Too-arll-oh-mee', 'Twa-lo-mee' or 'Too-all-um-nee') is a Native American name. All the facilities at Tuolumne Meadows are seasonal, and are open from around the end of June to about the middle of September. The following information refers to the main summer holiday season only.

There is a store open from 9am until 6pm daily, and a post office (part of the same building) with opening hours of 9am to 4pm weekdays and 9am to 12pm Saturdays. It is essential to take account of these times if you are depending upon the food supplies here. There is also a take-away grill which sells hamburgers, chips and the like: this is open from 8am until 5pm. Take your fill of this fatty fast food as you will not have the opportunity to gorge yourself again until Reds Meadow Resort, over three days' hike from here.

In addition to the campground there is also Tuolumne Lodge for those wanting a bed for the night, but this may be booked up during the main season. Note that the lodge is over a mile from the centre of Tuolumne Meadows, but there is a free shuttle bus operating to and from the lodge during the main summer season, generally from early July to 8th September. Dinner is available at Tuolumne Lodge for both residents and non-residents, but it is essential to reserve a place for dinner (tel. 372-8413).

There is some confusion as to whether JMT and PCT Thru-Hikers and permit holders have to pay at Tuolumne Meadows Backpackers' Campground – enquire from a warden as to the current requirements. If payment is necessary then this is made by placing dollar notes (probably $5 per person) in the yellow envelope provided and

Mules carry provisions for some fortunate groups – this mule train is near Cathedral Pass heading towards Tuolumne Meadows

'posting' it in the special box, which you will find in the camping area. Note that only in an emergency is more than one night allowed at this campsite.

The only place to indulge in a hot shower in Tuolumne Meadows is at Tuolumne Lodge. Showers are available only between the hours of noon and 3.30pm, and a charge is made. But beware that during a long dry spell of weather (common during the summer in the High Sierra) in periods of water shortage, no showers are allowed. No showers are available on the campground.

The problem for the hot and foot-weary trekker is that Tuolumne Meadows' facilities are widely separated, from the visitor centre in the west to Tuolumne Lodge in the east. In the centre is the store/post office and take-away grill. The latter provides both lunch and dinner, and also serves breakfast, although not until 8am in the morning. Cooked breakfasts, cereals and pancakes are all on offer. There is also a hiking-gear shop in Tuolumne Meadows (attached to the garage, 100 yards west of the main store) where most items of gear can be bought. Dehydrated food, dried nuts, etc, can be bought in the village store, but the stock is not usually extensive. Water filters can usually be purchased in the store and in the gear shop.

For those wanting a little activity on their day off at Tuolumne Meadows there are two main options. Botanists will wish to explore the meadows themselves, as the area is famous for its abundance and variety of wild flowers. The prominent granite peak of Lembert Dome dominates the view to the north, and the more adventurous will wish to walk out towards this most impressive mountain to gain a closer view.

There are talks on various aspects of the Yosemite National Park given by a park ranger every evening during the main summer holiday season. These are held in the Dana Open Air Theatre located next to the backpackers' area of the campground. They usually last for about an hour, take place around a campfire and are well worth attending. There are also ranger-led walks of varying lengths and themes during the daytime: one of the short ones could fit nicely into a rest day. Similar walks are also held in the evening, starting usually around 9.15–9.30pm, on themes such as 'night-time active animals' and the 'stars of the night sky'.

DAY 4

Tuolumne Meadows to Upper Lyell Canyon

Total distance of stage:	9.5 miles
Cumulative distance from Yosemite:	40.8 miles
Total ascent for stage:	1200ft
Total descent for stage:	100ft
Cumulative ascent from Yosemite:	9200ft
Cumulative descent from Yosemite:	3550ft

Location	Height (ft)	Distance (Miles)	
		Sectional	Cumulative
Tuolumne Meadows Campsite	8620	0	0
Rafferty Creek Trail	8720	1.7	1.7
JMT/Ireland Lake Trail Junction	8850	3.7	5.4
Upper Lyell Canyon camping area (Lyell Bridge/Lyell Fork)	9670	4.1	9.5

Map: Harrison Map Sheet 12

There is easy walking for much of the day, with the only significant climb being at the end of the stage. Lyell Canyon is an absolutely beautiful, long, relatively flat but steep-sided mountain valley. The waters of Lyell river, which have gouged out the canyon over millions of years, are pristine pure and a favourite of wild-country anglers, who will probably outnumber walkers during your day in the valley. Savour the tranquility of the canyon and the gentleness of the terrain: tomorrow the grandeur

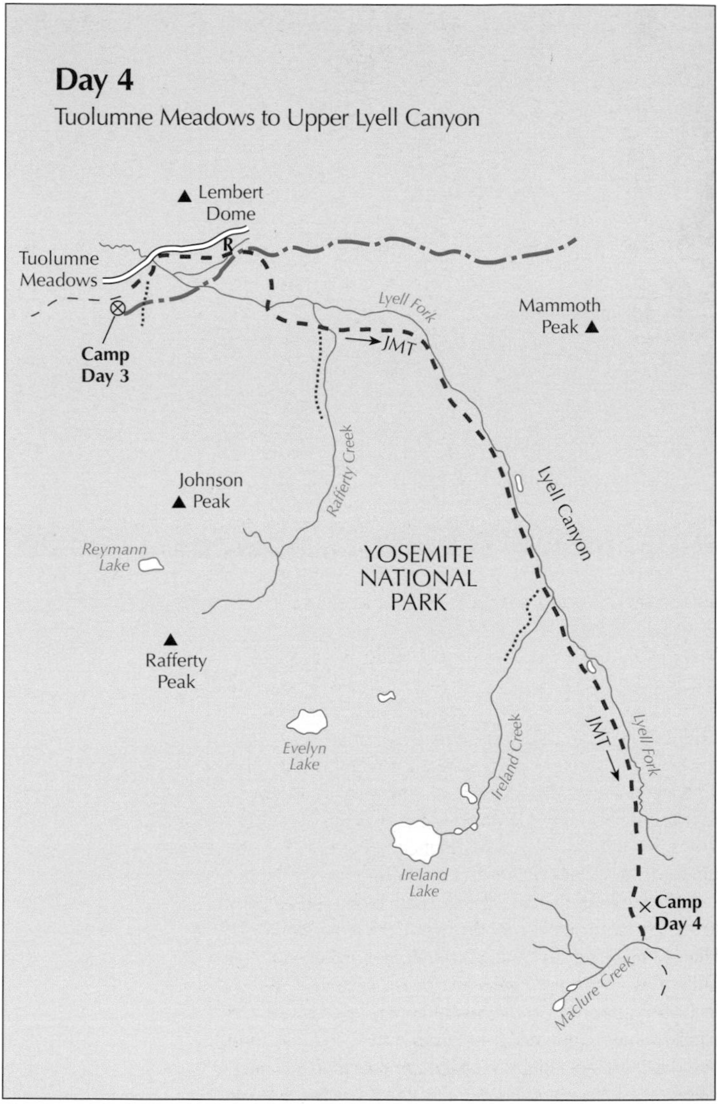

Day 4

Tuolumne Meadows to Upper Lyell Canyon

▲ Lembert
Dome

Tuolumne
Meadows

**Camp
Day 3**

Johnson
▲ Peak

Reymann
Lake

▲
Rafferty
Peak

Evelyn
Lake

Ireland
Lake

Lyell Fork

Mammoth
Peak ▲

→ JMT

Rafferty Creek

YOSEMITE
NATIONAL
PARK

Lyell Canyon

Ireland Creek

JMT
→

Lyell Fork

× Camp
Day 4

Maclure Creek

The start of the long trek up Lyell Canyon, east of Tuolumne Meadows

and savageness of the landscape will increase, as will the effort required to traverse it. The relatively low elevations of Yosemite are beginning to give way to the high peaks and passes that will be encountered further south.

Wander through the **Tuolumne Meadows campsite** to reach the shore of the River Lyell, which will be on your left. Follow the river. A trail waymark post indicating the PCT and JMT should soon be reached, and shortly after a wayside trail map is encountered. From this point it is 11.9 miles to the Donohue Pass along the Lyell Canyon Trail, which is co-incident with the JMT in this area of the Yosemite National Park (note that camping is prohibited until after about four miles out of Tuolumne).

Continue on the well-defined path alongside the river to reach a path junction. To the left is Tuolumne Meadows, High Sierra Camp and a ranger's station, but the John Muir Trail goes to the right, signposted to the Donohue Pass in 11.3 miles. The Trail leaves the banks of the river and climbs almost imperceptibly through the pine trees and over huge boulder slabs to reach another path junction. The way to Vogelsang heads off to the right, but the JMT

121

Fishing for your supper in Lyell Fork river, Lyell Canyon

keeps ahead. Within a few yards pass over a wooden bridge, and after a short while cross a wide open clearing in a forest. The Trail continues through more areas of scattered pines as its heads its way south.

Soon the dale widens and opens out. This broad, lush valley is an absolute delight, with the crystal-clear waters of the River Lyell flowing gently down from the distant high mountains. On either side are granite hillsides clad in pine trees. The walking is easy as the dusty path slowly makes its way upstream. This is bear country, the shallow river and the lush valley being to their liking, so you would be advised to go a little higher out of the valley before you camp. The Lyell Valley is a popular day and weekend hiking area and you will probably meet many other hikers on this stage of your journey. Several of them take rods to fish the Lyell, which is packed with trout – a great way to supplement your basic diet of dehydrated food.

The path rises slightly at a point where the river passes over some rock slides. Eventually you will reach a path junction with **Ireland Lake** (5.8 miles) off to the right. Ignore this, but continue ahead on the JMT. The Trail meanders in and out through trees heading higher and higher up the valley. Note the scratch marks and the torn bark on several of the trees around this area, evidence of bear activity. The route reaches an area known as Lyell Base Camp, a popular place with campers. However, a much better area to camp is to be found about a mile further on and 650ft higher at Lyell Bridge. To reach this point climb the well-constructed zig-zagging path until the trail flattens out and the river approaches. There are several **camping** spots on either side of the footbridge. This area is also known as Lyell Fork.

DAY 5

Upper Lyell Canyon via Donohue Pass and Island Pass to Thousand Island Lake

Total distance of stage:	9.7 miles
Cumulative distance from Yosemite:	50.5 miles
Total ascent for stage:	2200ft
Total descent for stage:	1950ft
Cumulative ascent from Yosemite:	11,400ft
Cumulative descent from Yosemite:	5500ft

Location	Height (ft)	Distance (miles)	
		Sectional	Cumulative
Upper Lyell Canyon camping area	9670	0	0
Donohue Pass	11,056	3.8	3.8
Rush Creek	9580	2.8	6.6
Island Pass	10,203	1.3	7.9
Thousand Island Lake camping area	9850	1.8	9.7

Maps: Harrison Map Sheets 12 and 11

Today sees an ascent to the first serious pass on the John Muir Trail. The Donohue Pass stands at 11,056ft and as such should not be underestimated, particularly

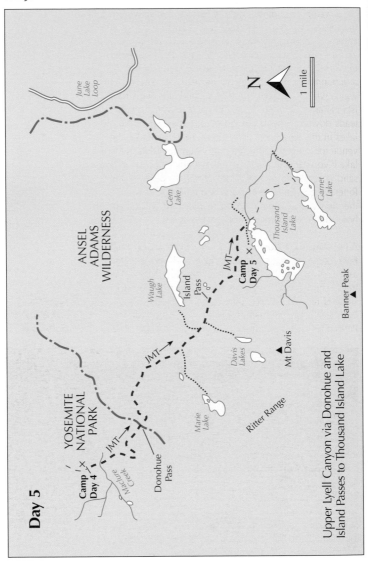

Day 5

Upper Lyell Canyon via Donohue and
Island Passes to Thousand Island Lake

if the weather conditions are not perfect. The view from the top of the pass is stunning and hints at the joys to come as one heads further along the JMT. At the pass you say goodbye to Yosemite National Park as you enter the Ansel Adams Wilderness. Here is a land of a myriad mountain tarns and larger high-level lakes, several of which will be passed en route. A second pass of the day, Island Pass, is a relatively easy obstacle to overcome, but leads down to one of the largest and most spectacular lakes in this wilderness area, Thousand Island Lake, the venue for tonight's wild camping. Count the islets in the lake if you can: there are very many of them, but a thousand is surely an exaggeration! The main peaks of the Ritter range, Banner Peak and Mount Ritter, dominate the view at this camping area; memories of your night here will no doubt remain for years to come.

After enjoying a hopefully bear-free night at the **Lyell Fork campsite** cross the footbridge and continue the ascent on a good path that climbs steadily through the trees. The treeline is reached at a small mountain tarn situated in a delightful alpine meadow beneath Mount Lyell (13,144ft), the highest peak in Yosemite National Park. This mountain also holds a small glacier in its

The Mount Ritter range seen from near the Donohue Pass

Banner Peak in evening shadow, seen from the camping area by Thousand Island Lake

corrie: although quite tiny, this is the largest glacier seen from the JMT.

The stream outlet from the tarn provides the first of many river crossings to be encountered as you progress along the JMT. Ahead lies the Donohue Pass, but to reach it requires a considerable sustained effort. The Trail first climbs to the right, heading towards the high mountains and snowfields/glacier, before descending to another mountain tarn, where there is another stream crossing. Note the many bore holes in the rocks at the side of the path; these were made to take the dynamite rods that blasted the rock to make the Trail. The final climb is eastwards amongst a jumble of rocks and boulders heading directly for the Donohue Pass. The top of the pass is at 11,050ft, the highest point so far reached on this trek. The next time an elevation of over 11,000ft will be reached will be at Muir Pass, probably about nine walking days further along the Trail.

The **Donohue Pass** marks the boundary between the Yosemite National Park and the Ansel Adams Wilderness. Those wishing to climb Donohue Peak from Donohue Pass will find that it is a simple ascent, although there is some boulder clambering at the top. Bid a sad farewell to Yosemite as you begin the descent eastwards to enter the next phase of your journey. The area where signposts mark the top of the pass and the Yosemite National Park/Ansel Adams Wilderness boundary is not the best place to make a stop. Instead continue for about another 100–150yds to a point just before the descent begins: this is a good viewpoint for the wilderness country that lies ahead.

The descent on the far side of the pass is fairly gentle, and within ½hr you should reach the first sparsely scattered tress and bushes. The moderate descent continues through the trees with fine views of alpine-style peaks and snowfields. The dramatic pointed peaks of the Ritter range (Banner Peak and its twin, Mount Ritter) dominate the view. The Trail descends to a major river crossing at Rush Creek. In dry conditions the crossing is very easy, but at times of spate this is a major obstacle, a serious river crossing.

On the far side of the river continue along the Trail, crossing two or three minor streams to reach a trail junction. The Rush Creek Trail to Glen Lake and Silver Lake turns left to immediately cross the river. However, the JMT takes the Pacific Crest Trail (PCT) ahead, signposted to Island Pass. Follow the latter, soon reaching a double log bridge over a stream: cross this and continue ahead to cross a second stream within 100yds, this one by means of stepping stones.

The path climbs to **Island Pass**, where the most beautiful view awaits the hiker. A mountain tarn with Mount Banner behind forms the perfect mountain photograph. Unlike the Donohue Pass, Island Pass is not well defined, being long and flat-topped, but soon the Trail begins its descent. Follow it until it reaches a JMT/PCT trail junction near the outlet of Thousand Island Lake. Note that camping is not permitted for ½ mile either side of the lake outlet. Some good sites will be found by following the northern shore of the lake for about ¼ mile and then climbing upwards for about 60ft towards the trees. This is a fantastic spot to **camp** for the night, with the superb backdrop of Thousand Island Lake and Mount Banner.

DAY 6

Thousand Island Lake to the Devil's Postpile

Total distance of stage:	16.2 miles
Cumulative distance from Yosemite:	66.7 miles
Total ascent for stage:	1800ft
Total descent for stage:	4100ft
Cumulative ascent from Yosemite:	13,200ft
Cumulative descent from Yosemite:	9600ft

Location	Height (ft)	Distance (miles)	
		Sectional	Cumulative
Thousand Island Lake camping area	9850	0	0
Emerald Lake	9900	1.0	1.0
Garnet Lake Outlet Stream	9650	1.7	2.7
Shadow Lake	8800	3.5	6.2
Gladys Lake	9600	2.3	8.5
Johnson Meadows	8140	5.2	13.7
Devil's Postpile Campsite	7580	2.5	16.2

Maps: Harrison Map Sheets 11 and 10

Since Tuolumne Meadows the JMT has been co-incident with its bigger brother, the Pacific Crest Trail (PCT). But at Thousand Island Lake the JMT and PCT part company with each other for the day, not being reunited until the Devil's Postpile is reached at the end of the stage. The PCT follows the south-western slopes of the San Joaquin range to the north-east of the JMT, which threads its way though some of the best mountain lake country on the whole of the Trail. Several lakes and tarns are passed on today's route, names that will trip off the tongue as you think back on this stage in the months and years to come: the tiny Emerald and Ruby lakes and the large Garnet Lake, with its amazing surrounding mountain views of the towering Ritter range. There are several stiff ascents and descents on the Trail as the route heads south-eastwards, reaching Shadow Lake, Rosalie Lake and then Gladys Lake before beginning a long descent through trees to Johnston Lake. From here it is relatively easy walking to the ranger station and Devil's Postpile Campground, but weary legs will carry the walker over these last few miles of the longest stage on the JMT.

Some walkers may wish to camp before the Devil's Postpile, and thus make today and tomorrow more even in length, but to do so would leave less time to inspect the fascinating Devil's Postpile and enjoy the luxury of a hot thermal bath *and* a cooked meal at Reds Meadow – all to be savoured tomorrow. The alternative is to take three days rather than two to get from Thousand Island Lake to Deer Creek, which is possible without carrying an excessive weight of food supplies, as a restaurant and store are available at Reds Meadow. The choice, as always, is yours.

From your overnight **campsite** return to the PCT/JMT junction and follow the JMT over the outlet stream of **Thousand Island Lake** by way of a log bridge. The path first passes to the right of a small lake (Emerald Lake) and then to the left of the larger Ruby Lake. After these two lakes the route climbs a low ridge by a series of zig-zags: this path should be in shadow provided an early start from camp was made. A descent follows towards **Garnet Lake**, another magical viewpoint for Mount Ritter. Like Thousand Island Lake before it, Garnet Lake is dotted with numerous tiny islets. There are also some camping spots at Garnet Lake, although the same restriction applies as at Thousand Island Lake – not within ½ mile of the outlet). The Trail descends to the crystal-clear waters of the lake, a favourite haunt of wild-country fishermen, to follow its north-east shore and cross its outlet stream by a log footbridge, which hopefully still possesses its protective handrail.

Once over the footbridge be sure to take the JMT footpath to the right, now following the opposite (south-

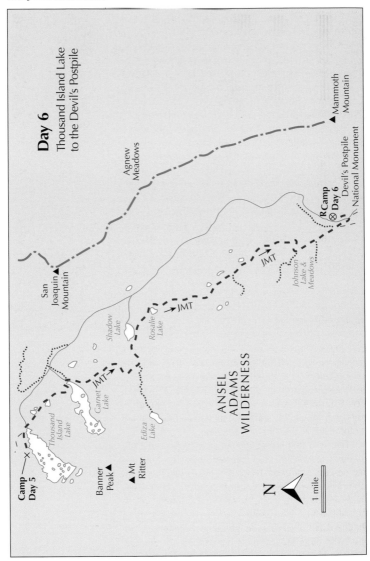

Day 6

Thousand Island Lake
to the Devil's Postpile

Mammoth
Mountain

Agnew
Meadows

R Camp
⊗ Day 6
Devil's Postpile
National Monument

San
Joaquin
Mountain

JMT

Johnson
Lake &
Meadows

Shadow
Lake

Rosalie
Lake

JMT

Camp
Day 5

Thousand
Island
Lake

JMT

Garnet
Lake

Ediza
Lake

ANSEL
ADAMS
WILDERNESS

Banner
Peak

Mt
Ritter

N

1 mile

east) shore of Garnet Lake. Mount Ritter with its small glaciers and snowfields still dominates this mountain wonderland. The path follows the lakeside for a while before beginning a zig-zagging climb above it to reach a col from where a new set of views towards the south greet you, mountains and cols that will be encountered at closer quarters in the days to come.

The Trail then descends by a zig-zagging path to an alpine-style meadow. From here there is a long further descent of around 1000ft down to a wide wooden footbridge over a broad, fast-flowing river, which feeds Shadow Lake. Cross this bridge and continue along the path, which soon drops a little to gain the shore of **Shadow Lake**. Here is a delightful spot for lunch and/or a swim (note that camping is prohibited by Shadow Creek and Lake).

Campers on the shore of Lake Garnet, with Banner Peak and Mount Ritter forming a magnificent backdrop

131

The JMT leaves the shoreline to climb on an excellently engineered switchback path up through a dense pine forest to reach a saddle. Pass over this to descend to Rosalie Lake. The path skirts this beautiful, deep, blue stretch of water for a while before climbing once more to reach the next high point, just below which lies yet another lake, Gladys Lake. The JMT passes to the right of this lake to climb one more time. However, this ascent is a very short and gentle one, a fact that will no doubt be welcome, as the day will by now probably be well advanced.

From here it is all descent. A long section of downhill follows through the trees towards Johnson Meadows. A couple of reed-filled tarns (Trinity Lakes) are passed on your left during this section. This seemingly endless descent finishes with a few zig-zags to deposit the walker at **Johnson Meadows**. Here turn left on the JMT, signposted to Reds Meadow. The path has a surface of pumice, which is very dusty. It leads to a ford and log footbridge over a river. Cross this and continue until you reach the boundary of the Devil's Postpile/Reds Meadow Area. Follow the signs for the ranger station: the path leads to a footbridge over a major river. After crossing this bridge the JMT turns immediately to the right. However, those making for the **campground** should take the left turn to walk on a track for about ¼ mile to the ranger station. Check in here before making your way to the backpackers' area of the campsite (Section B3), a few minutes' walk from the building ($14 per person per night in 2010, the best site in the entire campground is on the top of a hill overlooking the river, but room for only one or two tents). Note that normally it is unnecessary to treat or filter water either at this campsite or at the nearby Bathhouse Campsite ($16 per person per night in 2006).

DAY 7

The Devil's Postpile
via Reds Meadow to Deer Creek

Total distance of stage:	9.0 miles
Cumulative distance from Yosemite:	75.7 miles
Total ascent for stage:	1700ft
Total descent for stage:	150ft
Cumulative ascent from Yosemite:	14,900ft
Cumulative descent from Yosemite:	9750ft

Location	Height (ft)	Distance (miles)	
		Sectional	Cumulative
Devil's Postpile Campsite	7580	0	0
Reds Meadow Campsite and hot thermal showers	7600	1.9	1.9
Reds Meadow Resort	7750	1.5	3.4
Upper Crater Meadow	8920	4.5	7.9
Deer Creek camping area	9150	1.1	9.0

Maps: Harrison Map Sheets 10 and 9

Today is a relatively easy and short stage, but full of interest and enjoyment. First it offers the chance to inspect a United States national monument, the Devil's Postpile, a remarkable natural feature (see below). The next stop provides the opportunity of a hot bath, but a bath like no other, in a thermal bathtub. Finally, a visit to Reds Meadow Resort offers the chance to eat some real food and rest thoroughly before tackling a climb back up into the hills to camp beside a woodland stream. A day to savour. It would be possible to have another rest day in the Reds Meadow/Devil's Postpile area, either staying at the Devil's Postpile Campsite for a second night or moving on just a little to the Bathhouse

133

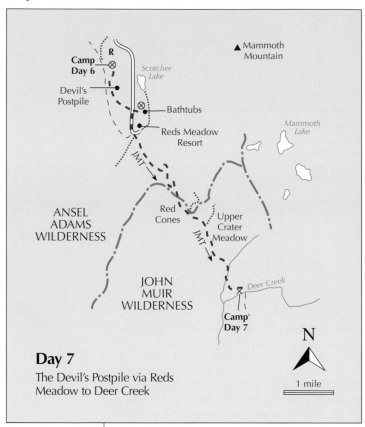

Day 7
The Devil's Postpile via Reds
Meadow to Deer Creek

Campsite, and perhaps also visiting the nearby Rainbow
Falls and Soda Springs (see below).

Retrace your steps southwards from the **campsite**/ranger
station to the footbridge, but this time do not cross it.
Instead continue south, signposted to the Devil's Postpile
and 'John Muir South'. Walk ahead until you reach the
signpost indicating the 'Top of the Postpile'. Leave your
backpacks here to walk uphill and examine from the top

the hexagonal, pentagonal and square basalt columns that form the **Devil's Postpile**.

After you have seen enough of this amazing natural site return to your sacs and continue south, uphill and downhill. On reaching a further signpost take the path signposted to Rainbow Falls. At the next junction turn left as indicated to Rainbow Falls and Reds Meadow. Cross a stream by a log footbridge and immediately turn left on a path signposted to Reds Meadow. At the main road turn left and continue for about 50yds and then go right to enter a campground. Walk through this to its end, where you will find the **Bath-house**. Here there are free hot thermal showers, all enclosed in cubicles. A must! Take full benefit of washing both body and clothes. You will not get such an opportunity again until reaching the Vermilion Resort at the end of Day 9.

After a wash and brush-up the next stop is the Reds Meadow store and diner for a much needed food top-up. Walk back through the campground to the main road and turn left, south, along it. Follow this road, ignoring the Rainbow Falls trailhead turn-off to the right, and follow the road as it then enters the **Reds Meadow Resort**. (Alternatively to reach the Red's Meadow store from the Bath-house, there is a cut-through trail on the right 10yds before the bathhouse itself; this goes directly to the store rather than retracing your steps back through the campground and following the road.) The road soon swings to the left (north) to reach the café (breakfasts and lunch!) next to the general store. Take plenty of time here to rest and recuperate and fill up on the calories that your body has no doubt been craving for days. The day is only a short one, with a relatively easy afternoon walk to Deer Creek, where you will make camp for the night. So enjoy your rest and food at Reds Meadow Resort (note that the resort has one large walk-in backpackers' campsite, next to all the vehicles; the overnight fee was $18 in 2008).

After you have taken your fill and bought any necessary additional food supplies from the store, leave Reds Meadow Resort. From the café/store area climb for about a minute to reach a cross-path: turn right on this, heading southwards and immediately to the right of the stables

The Mulehouse Café at the Reds Meadow resort, a welcome site for many hungry backpackers

or 'corral'. After 200yds, when the path forks, take the uphill (left) fork signed 'PCT South' (the right fork is signed 'Rainbow Falls'). Follow the Trail uphill, at first through an area that was severely burned in 1992 (the cause was lightening). Then an area of mature trees is entered, and a couple of small streams are crossed. The Trail is superbly angled in a series of very wide loops, and height is slowly but easily gained.

Eventually a high point on the Trail is reached at a major junction just before a river crossing. Here a path heads off to the left for Mammoth Pass to the north-east. Unless you require the facilities offered by the Mammoth Lake resort ignore this trail but instead descend for a few metres to cross the river. At this point you leave the Ansel Adams Wilderness to enter the John Muir Wilderness area. The JMT/PCT soon climbs again, eventually levelling to reach an open meadow, known as **Upper Crater Meadow**.

A sign should be located in this pleasant meadow area, indicating a further 2 miles to Deer Creek Crossing, and informing you that you have walked 4 miles since leaving Reds Meadow. Cross a small earthen bridge

Devil's Postpile

Protected as a national monument, the Devil's Postpile is an 800-acre site of basalt columns with three to seven sides and up to 60ft in height. They were formed relatively recently in geological terms, no more than 100,000 years ago, from cooling, cracking and shrinking lava, and exposed by moving ice in the last Ice Age around 10,000 years ago. There are few places on earth to see such phenomena, but some visitors may have seen basaltic columns of this nature in Fingal's Cave in Scotland and on the Giant's Causeway in Ireland. The Devil's Postpile is popular with tourists, who can easily reach this accessible area by road from Mammoth Lakes.

Rainbow Falls and Soda Springs

These are not included in the walk, but are close enough to fit in your itinerary. Rainbow Falls is a dramatic waterfall, 101ft in height, on the Middle Fork of the San Joaquin river. The Soda Springs, located on San Joaquin river gravel bar north of the Postpile, are cold, highly carbonated, mineralised springs.

Reds Meadow

Reds Meadow Resort opens about 22nd June and closes mid-September, depending on the weather. There is a phone, mailbox, stamps and plenty of food both cooked in the café and for sale in the general store. The Mulehouse Café's opening hours are from 7am to 7pm. Don't miss the wonderful food here: ham and cheeseburgers for main course and superb homemade fruit pies and ice cream for desert, and always service with a smile. For those not wishing to walk there is a free shuttle-bus service operating between the Devil's Postpile Ranger Station and Reds Meadow between 7.30am and 6.20pm. This bus service also takes hikers to the town of Mammoth Lakes.

over a stream in the middle of Upper Crater Meadow and cross another small stream at the far end of the clearing before entering woods and climbing gently once more. Continue on the well-defined, often dusty, pumice-covered path through the trees. After a couple of miles you will reach Deer Creek Crossing, indicated by a signboard on a tree, a few yards before the stream. This is the recommended spot for **camping**, as there is no more water for 6 miles.

137

Basalt columns of the Devil's Postpile

DAY 8

Deer Creek to Tully Hole/Cascade Valley Junction

Total distance of stage:	12.3 miles
Cumulative distance from Yosemite:	88.0 miles
Total ascent for stage:	2050ft
Total descent for stage:	2050ft
Cumulative ascent from Yosemite:	16,950ft
Cumulative descent from Yosemite:	11,800ft

Location	Height (ft)	Distance (miles)	
		Sectional	Cumulative
Deer Creek camping area	9150	0	0
JMT/Duck Lake Trail Junction	10,480	5.9	5.9
Purple Lake	9930	2.0	7.9
Lake Virginia	10,320	1.9	9.8
Tully Hole	9600	1.4	11.2
JMT/Cascade Valley Trail Junction	9120	1.1	12.3

Maps: Harrison Map Sheets 9 and 8

Be sure to load up with plenty of water for the first half of today's route as none will be found for many miles. The first section of the Trail follows a well-defined but dusty track over ground pumice. More beautiful mountain lakes are encountered today. After passing a side-trail to the large Duck Lake the JMT reaches Purple Lake before climbing a gully beneath a huge broken rock face and reaching Lake Virginia, which is situated at over 10,000ft above sea level. A rocky, savage landscape is replaced by a verdant valley as numerous zig-zags take the walker down to Tully Hole. A camp here or a mile further down the valley is the last wilderness campsite before your well-earned rest day at Vermilion.

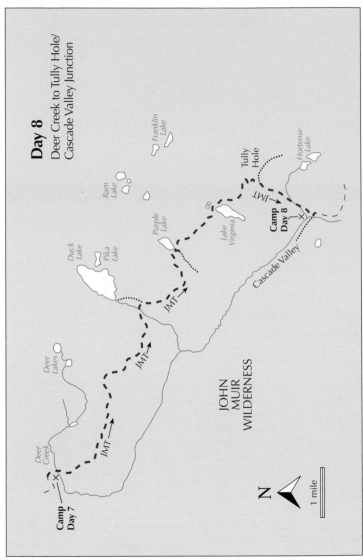

Day 8

Deer Creek to Tully Hole/
Cascade Valley Junction

Franklin
Lake

Ram
Lake

Tully
Hole

Hortense
Lake

JMT

Purple
Lake

8

Lake
Virginia

**Camp
Day 8**

Duck
Lake

Pika
Lake

JMT

Cascade Valley

Deer
Lakes

JMT

JMT

JOHN MUIR
WILDERNESS

Deer
Creek

**Camp
Day 7**

N

1 mile

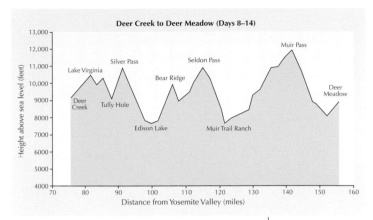

Deer Creek to Deer Meadow (Days 8–14)

Cross Deer Creek and follow the well-defined, pumice-surfaced, dusty track upward through the trees. As is usually the case with the JMT, this path is well graded. For a while there are no views, but higher up the trail views of a high rocky ridge open out to the right. The path levels and then contours for a couple of miles or more around the mountainside, eventually turning north-eastwards with a creek over to the right. Cross this creek and climb for about 150ft to reach a trail junction. Left is a path that leads to Duck Pass and Lake. Ignore this, but instead turn right, south, to continue along the PCT/JMT heading for Purple Lake.

The path climbs for a while over a shoulder before contouring around the hillside, with ever improving views of high mountains across the valley. A descent leads to a trail junction for Ram Lake. Ignore this path and walk down to the shore of **Purple Lake**, an ideal spot for lunch. Walk around the lake following the signpost to Lake Virginia on the PCT/JMT. (Virginia Lake is also an excellent place to camp, although it can be quite windy, so that it is best to camp in the shelter of the trees. Cross the outlet stream of the lake (this could be difficult if the water is in spate). From the opposite shore of the stream the Trail climbs steeply by

Near the col between Purple Lake and Lake Virginia

a series of zig-zags (or switchbacks, as the Americans say) beneath a huge broken rock face to reach a wide, boulder-strewn col.

Enjoy the shade of the trees at the highest point before starting an easy descent to **Lake Virginia**. Pass to the left of the lake, fording the inlet stream (possibly difficult when in spate) and follow the undulating path along the northern shore of the lake. The mountain setting around Lake Virginia is magnificent. Continue along the path until suddenly the verdant **Tully Hole Meadow** comes into sight far below. This meadow is reached by a superbly constructed path that descends by a series of well-graded wide zig-zags. On reaching the meadows follow the path to the right, into the trees, and soon reach a trail junction. To the left is the path leading to McGee Pass. Ignore this and continue ahead alongside a fast-flowing mountain stream (Fish Creek), the water tumbling and cascading over rocky boulders and mini-

waterfalls. After about a mile the Trail crosses this torrent over a sturdy metal footbridge.

A few hundred yards later a trail junction is met: to the right is a path to **Cascade Valley**. Ignore this and continue ahead on the JMT/PCT Trail. But about 50yds before the Cascade Valley Junction is the recommended **camping area** at the end of today's stage. Here there is a rough but perfectly adequate site for an overnight camp on the right of the path: there is space for about three tents. Water should be found in the stream which is located on the JMT/PCT trail about 30yds after the Cascade Valley Junction.

Better camping spots may be found at Tully Hole, and there is certainly an abundance of water there. However, to stop for the night at Tully Hole will add an hour to tomorrow's walk, and it is very important to catch the afternoon ferry at the end of tomorrow's stage.

Hikers on the JMT south-east of Lake Virginia

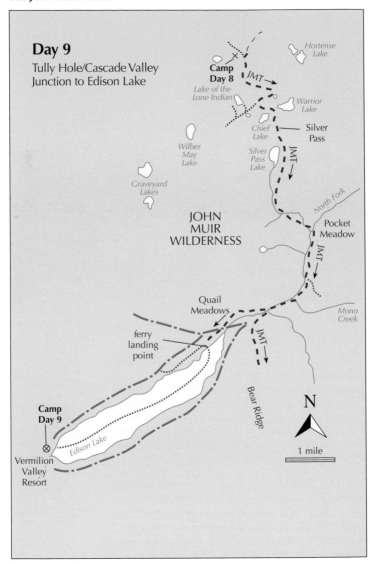

Day 9

Tully Hole/Cascade Valley
Junction to Edison Lake

Hortense Lake

Camp Day 8

JMT

Lake of the Lone Indian

Warrior Lake

Chief Lake

Silver Pass

Silver Pass Lake

JMT

Wilber May Lake

Graveyard Lakes

North Fork

JOHN MUIR WILDERNESS

Pocket Meadow

JMT

Quail Meadows

Mono Creek

ferry landing point

JMT

Camp Day 9

Bear Ridge

N

Edison Lake

1 mile

Vermilion Valley Resort

DAY 9

Tully Hole/Cascade Valley
Junction via Silver Pass to Edison Lake

Total distance of stage:	11.8 miles
Cumulative distance from Yosemite:	99.8 miles
Total ascent for stage:	1850ft
Total descent for stage:	3150ft
Cumulative ascent from Yosemite:	18,800ft
Cumulative descent from Yosemite:	14,950ft

Location	Height (ft)	Distance (miles)	
		Sectional	Cumulative
JMT/Cascade Valley Trail Junction	9120	0	0
Squaw Lake	10,300	2.2	2.2
Silver Pass	10,900	1.2	3.4
JMT/Mott Lake Trail Junction (Pocket Meadow)	8880	4.0	7.4
JMT/Mono Creek Trail Junction	8320	1.2	8.6
JMT/Edison Lake Trail Junction (Quail Meadows)	7820	1.3	9.9
Mono Creek ferry pick-up (Edison Lake)	7650	1.9	11.8

Map: Harrison Map Sheet 8

The day commences with a climb to a high pass, Silver Pass, at 10,900ft. The area to the northern side of the pass abounds with picturesque mountain tarns, all with names derived from the Native American people: Lake of the Lone Indian, Squaw Lake, Warrior Lake, Chief Lake and Papoose Lake. South of the pass the Trail passes another lake which bears the same name as the pass, Silver Pass Lake – an uninspiring name, but inspiring country. A long descent and possibly a difficult river crossing lead to a forested valley that descends via a series of meadows to

Heavily laden hiker on the JMT south of Silver Pass

a major trail junction. The JMT climbs to the south-east onto Bear Ridge, but to miss the delights of the Vermilion Resort, which really is an essential part of hiking the John Muir or Pacific Crest trails, would be sacrilege indeed. Besides, you will almost certainly have food supplies waiting for collection at Vermilion. So leave the JMT for a while here and head off to the south-west for Edison Lake and its twice-daily ferry to Vermilion Valley Resort.

From the Cascade Valley Junction the JMT path climbs almost immediately. An early start is recommended so that the initial part of the ascent, up to the first lake, is accomplished while the mountainside is in shadow. Once again the Trail is well graded. Numerous zig-zags lead the walker up the valley, sometimes over smooth slabs, to reach an upper rocky basin in which is located Squaw Lake. Cross the outlet stream of this lake and continue westwards to reach a junction. To the right is the path to the **Lake of the Lone Indian** and the Goodale Pass. However, the JMT path bends to the left. From this point there is just over a mile and almost 400ft of ascent to the Silver Pass. The path levels for a while to approach two small tarns and the much larger **Chief Lake**. Finally it climbs again to the east and the south to reach the wooden board which marks the summit of **Silver Pass** (10,900ft).

The top of the pass marks the boundary of the Inyo National Forest and the Sierra National Forest. Be sure to take a few paces to the west from the wooden notice board in order to see the marvellous view of the area's many lakes: Squaw, Chief, Warrior, Papoose. Having enjoyed the stupendous view from the pass leave the Inyo National Forest by heading south into the Sierra National Forest, gently downhill among a superb mountainscape. Pass to the left of **Silver Pass Lake**. After a couple of miles the Trail crosses Silver Pass Creek. Soon after this the path plunges down into the main valley by a long series of zig-zags. Note the enormous slabs of polished granite over to the left, the result of glacial activity during the last Ice Age. Near the bottom of the zig-zags reach and cross a boulder-filled creek. It is an easy crossing during a dry summer,

The Edison Queen approaching Mono Creek ferry pick-up point

and even in normal conditions the ford should present few problems. However, when the river is in spate, particularly common in early season when the snow is melting above, this can be an extremely dangerous crossing.

A few yards after the creek the trail junction is reached to Mott Lake at **Pocket Meadow**. Ignore this, but continue ahead following the sign for Edison Lake. Continue the descent. After 1.4 miles reach another track junction, that to Mono Pass. Ignore this path as well, continuing ahead on the JMT, again signposted to Edison Lake. After about ¾ mile the path crosses another stream and continues with the valley river to the left. In a further ½ mile a trail junction is reached at **Quail Meadows**. The JMT/PCT turns left here, signposted to the Seldon Pass. However, the major rest and recuperation centre of the JMT now beckons, and most will want to make the most of the facilities on offer at Vermilion Resort. So for the moment leave the John Muir Trail here, continuing ahead for about 2 miles to the Edison Lake **ferry pick-up point** (ie. follow the path ahead for about 1.7 miles to reach a path junction where you turn left as indicated for the Mono Creek ferry pick-up point). At the time of writing the ferry arrives here during the main summer hiking season at 9.45am and at 4.45pm (see 'Rest Day – Vermilion Valley Resort', below). The ferry goes directly to Vermilion Valley Resort.

Note

During periods of drought Edison Lake dries up considerably, such that the ferry may not be able to operate. At such times it will be necessary to follow a trail above the northern shore of the lake to Vermilion Resort (see Harrison Map Sheet 8), a distance of over 4 miles. However, note also that if these drought conditions come towards the end of the summer season, Vermilion Resort may close early for the year.

REST DAY

Vermilion Valley Resort (VVR)

By the time you reach Edison Lake you will have walked around 100 miles and so fully deserve a rest day at Vermilion Resort. There is a twice-daily ferry (the *Edison Queen*) which operates across Edison Lake during the main summer hiking season, particularly for JMT/PCT and other wilderness hikers, enabling them to spend time at the Vermilion Resort and return to the Trail after plenty of rest and recuperation. The service normally runs from 15th June to 30th September, but the beginning and end of the season are often affected by adverse weather, so causing a late start to the service or an early curtailment. The details of the ferry service are usually as follows (but JMT hikers are advised to check on this before starting the Trail) – note that in some exceptionally dry years, at the end of the season, the lake can dry up considerably, in which case a small relief ferry will probably be run from further along the lake, where there is sufficient water to operate; information on the status of the ferry is easily gleaned from approaching hikers coming from the lake, or from Rangers).

FERRY DETAILS

- Ferry from Mono Creek pick-up point: 9.45am and 4.45pm
- Ferry from Vermilion Resort: 9am and 4pm
- A one-way journey takes around 20mins.
- There is a moderate charge for the service ($16 return in 2008).

The Vermilion Valley Resort welcomes all, but particular attention is given to wilderness walkers, especially JMT and PCT Thru-Hikers. The owners do their utmost to give the long-distance hiker a wonderful rest in friendly surroundings and supply huge quantities of first-rate homemade food at reasonable prices. It is also the only re-supply point on the JMT which charges a reasonable sum for collecting and keeping food supplies for long-distance hikers; their charges for this service are much lower than those of Reds Meadow and Muir Trail Ranch. Staying at Vermilion has become almost an obligatory part of the JMT or PCT experience. You are sure to take away many happy memories of your stay here.

VERMILION VALLEY RESORT FACILITIES

Although conditions and facilities may change it is likely that the following will apply.

- Accommodation is in tented cabins, and the first night is free in tented cabins (subject to availability) or in your own tent. The tented cabins are equipped with bed mattresses. The second and any subsequent nights cost $12 per person.

- The food is excellent, with breakfast, lunch and dinner available (moreover, the first drink is 'on the house'). Be sure to eat as many calories as possible here. It is your last chance to eat 'real' food until the end of the JMT, 12 days and over 130 miles from here (the restaurant is open from 7am to 8pm).

- An integral part of Vermilion is a store with plenty of backpacking and other food for sale, as well as hiking and camping gear (store opening times are from 7am to 9pm).

- There is usually a 'hiker's barrel' where excess food/gear can be left for other hikers. Take only what you really need from this.

- Washing machines are available for laundry ($5 per wash in 2008, including detergent).

- Hot showers cost $6 in 2008.

- A phone is available, as is internet, but via satellite and so very expensive.

- The preferred system for payment is to put everything on a 'tab' and pay by card or cash when you leave. You may well accumulate quite a bill, but you won't be spending money again until your long trek is over!

Note should be made of Butch Wiggs, the owner of the Vermilion Valley Resort, who died unexpectedly at an early age in 2001. Butch and his wife, Peggy, had built up the VVR in just a few years into a stopover place for tired and recuperating hikers that was renowned all over the States, and even further afield, for its hospitality and friendliness. He created a unique atmosphere, providing a memorable stay for all who visited. He is sorely missed.

When you leave VVR you begin the long trek southwards through an extensive wilderness. Vermilion was the last chance for a complete rest with good, cooked food and other home comforts; the next time you will have such facilities will be in Lone Pine at the end of your adventure.

DAY 10

Edison Lake to Rosemarie Meadow

Total distance of stage:	12.3 miles
Cumulative distance from Yosemite:	112.1 miles
Total ascent for stage:	3350ft
Total descent for stage:	1050ft
Cumulative ascent from Yosemite:	22,150ft
Cumulative descent from Yosemite:	16,000ft

It is two days from Edison Lake to Muir Trail Ranch, which lies to the south of another major pass on the JMT, Seldon Pass. Its height at 10,900ft is identical to that of Silver Pass, which was crossed a few days ago in order to reach Vermilion. But it is too far to reach Seldon Pass from Edison Lake in one day, and much of today's stage is amongst trees on the long approach march. The morning will be taken up with a long climb onto Bear Ridge. Other hikers at Vermilion have no doubt told you how 'awesome' the climb is, but taken steadily it is a relatively easy

Note for 2010 Reprint: Some adverse reports have been made in recent years as to the 'hiker friendliness' of the Vermilion Valley Resort, the cost of the facilities, range of food on offer, and the character of some of the clients. VVR is now under new ownership. After contacting several JMT trekkers who have visited the resort from 2005 to 2008 it appears that many hikers still have an enjoyable experience at VVR, and find the cost not unreasonable for such a remote establishment. Some clients have suggested that an itemised bill be requested when settling your account at the end of your stay.

Location	Height (ft)	Distance (miles)	
		Sectional	Cumulative
Mono Creek ferry pick-up (Edison Lake)	7650	0	0
JMT/Edison Lake Trail Junction (Quail Meadows)	7820	1.9	1.9
JMT/Bear Ridge Trail Junction	9920	4.4	6.3
JMT/Bear Creek Trail Junction	8960	1.8	8.1
Upper Bear Creek Meadows	9500	3.3	11.4
Rosemarie Meadow	9960	0.9	12.3

Maps: Harrison Map Sheets 8 and 7

ascent. The first of the high peaks of the south will come into view today, the 12,349ft Mount Hooper, which lies to the west of the Seldon Pass. Bear Creek is followed for many miles to Upper Bear Creek Meadows and then its west fork leads up to Rosemarie Meadow, where good camping spots will be found to spend the night.

When you have recovered at Vermilion from the stresses and strains of the first nine days or so on the Trail, it is time to move on. Take the morning **ferry** from Vermilion across Edison Lake to land back at Mono Creek. Walk the 2 miles or so back to the junction with the JMT, where you left off the Trail to detour to Vermilion. Turn right to follow the path signposted to Seldon Pass. After about 100yds the Trail crosses a wood/metal/concrete footbridge over the Mono river. So begins the long, hard climb up to Bear Ridge.

The climb onto Bear Ridge should not be dreaded: although you will not be able to make an early start because the ferry from Vermilion does not leave until 9.00am, the entire climb takes place beneath the shade of good tree cover, so the temperature should be relatively cool. Furthermore your blood sugar levels should be well up because of the amount of good food you have eaten at Vermilion!

The Trail does not immediately begin its ascent, but for 5mins or so it remains level and even descends slightly

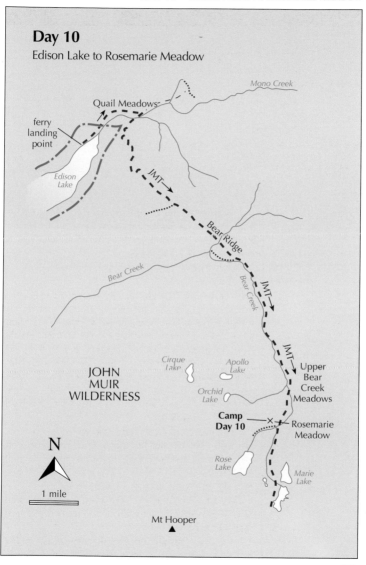

Day 10

Edison Lake to Rosemarie Meadow

Mono Creek

Quail Meadows

ferry landing point

Edison Lake

JMT

Bear Ridge

Bear Creek

Bear Creek

JMT

JMT

Cirque Lake

Apollo Lake

Orchid Lake

Upper Bear Creek Meadows

JOHN MUIR WILDERNESS

Camp Day 10

Rosemarie Meadow

N

Rose Lake

Marie Lake

1 mile

Mt Hooper

Distant Mount Hooper seen from the JMT on Bear Ridge

at one point. After crossing a small stream the steep climb begins in earnest. A long succession of zig-zags on the well-graded path leads the walker on the ascent of over 2000ft up onto **Bear Ridge** (the official number of switchbacks is 57!). After these seemingly endless zig-zags the path eventually straightens and levels to head south-east along the wooded ridge, just below the 10,000ft contour line. After a while the path begins to descend slightly and soon reaches a path junction indicating 'Edison Lake West End'. Note that this trail, the Bear Ridge Trail, would be an alternative to taking the ferry from Vermilion back to Mono Creek: it is 5.7 miles long from this junction back to Vermilion. This point is shown as Bear Ridge Trail Junction on the Harrison *John Muir Trail Map-Pack*.

Continue ahead along the JMT, signposted to Seldon Pass. The path soon commences a fairly steep descent, and before long superb mountain views open out to the right: note the impressive Mount Hooper (12,349ft). Continue along the path, crossing several small streams to reach the junction with Bear Creek Trail. Ignore this and, as before, continue ahead, following Bear Creek up the valley. The water in the creek slides over rocks and tumbles down waterfalls. Eventually the trail reaches the junction to Lake

Italy. Ignore this, keeping ahead on the JMT up the valley, still following signposts to Seldon Pass. Slowly head up the rocky valley, crossing two major tributaries of Bear Creek in quick succession, to reach another trail junction at **Upper Bear Creek Meadows**. The path to the left leads to Seven Gables Lakes, but ignore this to follow the Pacific Crest Trail ahead. Almost immediately cross a stream by stepping stones and then climb on a rocky and dusty path for a total of about 500ft of ascent. At the end of the climb the Trail emerges at **Rosemarie Meadow**, your destination for the day. Cross the stream and in a few yards you will reach an excellent **camping area**.

DAY 11

*Rosemarie Meadow via
Seldon Pass to the Muir Trail Ranch*

Total distance of stage:	9.5 miles
Cumulative distance from Yosemite:	121.6 miles
Total ascent for stage:	1050ft
Total descent for stage:	3350ft
Cumulative ascent from Yosemite:	23,200ft
Cumulative descent from Yosemite:	19,350ft

Location	Height (ft)	Distance (miles)	
		Sectional	Cumulative
Rosemarie Meadow	9960	0	0
Seldon Pass	10,900	2.9	2.9
Sallie Keyes Lakes	10,250	2.1	5.0
JMT/Muir Trail Ranch Path Junction	8440	3.4	8.4
Muir Trail Ranch	7650	1.1	9.5

Map: Harrison Map Sheet 7

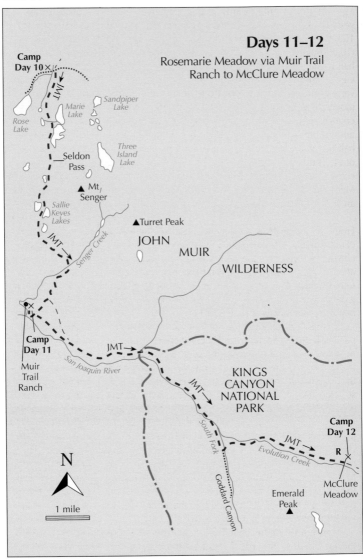

Days 11–12

Rosemarie Meadow via Muir Trail
Ranch to McClure Meadow

Camp
Day 10

JMT

Rose
Lake

Marie
Lake

Sandpiper
Lake

Seldon Pass

Three
Island
Lake

Sallie
Keyes
Lakes

▲ Mt
Senger

Senger Creek

▲ Turret Peak

JOHN   MUIR

WILDERNESS

JMT

Camp
Day 11

Muir
Trail
Ranch

San Joaquin River

JMT

KINGS
CANYON
NATIONAL
PARK

JMT

South Fork

Goddard Canyon

Camp
Day 12

R

JMT

Evolution Creek

McClure
Meadow

Emerald
Peak ▲

N

1 mile

Most of the ascent towards Seldon Pass was made yesterday, so it is a relatively easy ascent of around 1000ft to the top of the pass this morning. Seldon Pass (10,900ft) is the last of the great passes in the northern half of the JMT. From the top of the pass long-distance views remind you of the country that you have just traversed and beckon you forward towards the dramatic mountain wilderness of the southern Sierra. Glorious country lies south of the pass, but you will probably not wish to linger as today's stage is little more than a half-day walk, and you may have food parcels to sort out at Muir Trail Ranch for the 10 days of trekking to come. Also try to allow some time to enjoy the Blayney Meadows Hot Springs over the river from the camping area above Muir Trail Ranch.

From the **campsite** at Rosemarie Meadow there is a climb of a little less than 1000ft to Seldon Pass. The path climbs gradually from the campsite, passing Marie Lake, after which the route takes several zig-zags to reach the top of **Seldon Pass** at 10,900ft. As might be expected, great views abound. Be sure to enjoy them fully before beginning the long descent to Muir Trail Ranch.

The JMT descends to the south in glorious country, passing between **Sallie Keyes Lakes** before entering the treeline. The path rather unexpectedly, and disappointingly, climbs again for a short while before continuing the descent. After fording a creek (**Senger Creek**) the Trail soon begins a long zig-zagging descent into the valley, with little tree cover at first. On entering the trees and continuing the descent you will eventually reach a signpost indicating Piute Creek, Evolution Lake and Kings Canyon National Park to the left. This in fact is the John Muir Trail. Note that those not requiring the facilities of Muir Trail Ranch should turn left here: this path rejoins the route described in the guidebook where a second path from Muir Trail Ranch (used by those returning to the JMT from the ranch) meets the JMT.

Those heading for Muir Trail Ranch should ignore the JMT here to descend instead on the path ahead,

Optional detour to the summit of Mount Senger: An excellent scramble to a fine summit, it requires navigational and scrambling experience over steep and exposed terrain. Leave the JMT north of Seldon Pass to contour the slopes below the north-east peak, on granite slabs, keeping left of rock fragments and head up the rock ridge to the left of the scree chute. A fairly steep and exposed ridge of good but broken, granite scrambling, (Grade 1/2), leads to the western subsummit of this north-east peak. Descend south-east to a col, before heading up a ridge of sand and boulders, passing to right (south) of a rock tower and rejoining the ridgeline above, to the summit. Return to col, pass around the sub-summit and descend the scree chute. Cross some large rocks to rejoin the upward route.

Note that reports in 2005 suggest that Muir Trail Ranch now keep barrels containing surplus items of food, left by over-burdened hikers, which are normally available free of charge to other trekkers. One group reported that meals were easily obtainable at Muir Trail Ranch on request, but please do not rely on this; always make sure that you are carrying adequate supplies of lightweight food. If you have collected more food than you can fit in your bear canister, it is a good idea to return the surplus to the bear-proof shed at Muir Ranch for the night, collecting it in the morning before you leave.

signposted to Florence Lake (not signposted to Muir Trail Ranch at this point). After about ½ mile you will come to a sign that indicates Kings Canyon National Park to the left. This is the point to which you must return tomorrow in order to continue the Trail. But for now continue ahead following the sign for the MT Ranch (Muir Trail Ranch) and campground. Above the ranch is a track junction: continue ahead downhill for the **ranch** and your food caches. For the campground and Blayney Meadows Hot Springs (muddy) turn left. The camping area is on this side of the river; for the Blayney Meadows Hot Springs and nearby small clear lake for swimming (recommended), ford the river if the water is below your knees (it may be too high in early season). The Muir Trail Ranch is a classy rustic resort, quite different from that of Vermilion Valley Resort, but also much more expensive.

Today's stage is little more than a half-day walk, so you should have plenty of time on reaching Muir Trail Ranch to sort out your food supplies, relax in the Soda Springs and prepare for the second half of the JMT. You should make the most of this time of relaxation because you are about to enter the wildest sections of the Trail, with a succession of ever higher passes to overcome before arriving at the foot of continental North America's highest mountain. Unfortunately, because neither meals nor other food can normally be purchased at Muir Trail Ranch, you will probably not want to rest here a further day as this will use up valuable supplies that may well be needed in the days to come.

DAY 12

Muir Trail Ranch to McClure Meadow

Total distance of stage:	10.6 miles
Cumulative distance from Yosemite:	132.2 miles
Total ascent for stage:	2200ft
Total descent for stage:	200ft
Cumulative ascent from Yosemite:	25,400ft
Cumulative descent from Yosemite:	19,550ft

Location	Height (ft)	Distance (miles)	
		Sectional	Cumulative
Muir Trail Ranch	7650	0	0
Path Junction with JMT	7920	1.6	1.6
Boundary with Kings Canyon National Park (Piute Creek)	8080	1.7	3.3
Franklin Meadow	8450	3.8	7.1
Evolution Meadow	9280	1.2	8.3
McClure Meadow	9650	2.3	10.6

Maps: Harrison Map Sheets 7 and 6

Try to make the most of your relaxation time at Muir Trail Ranch, because from here on there are many miles and many passes to overcome on your long journey south in complete wilderness. There are no more roads, resorts or habitation of any sort, except for the occasional ranger station, from here until the end of the Trail at Whitney Portal. For many walkers this will be the first time that they have experienced such a huge expanse of unspoilt wilderness. Its crossing will surely be one of the highlights of your life.

Today is one of the few days that you won't be tackling one of the high passes on the route. From tomorrow it tends to be one day, one pass; and each one a little higher than the previous. Six of the next eight days include the crossing of a high mountain pass. But it is much too far to the next pass, Muir Pass, to cross it today. After rejoining the JMT, which you temporarily abandoned to reach Muir Trail Ranch yesterday, the Trail heads eastwards along the San Joaquin Valley to reach a large bridge over the Piute river. Once over this you have left the John Muir Wilderness area to enter the second of the three national parks through which the JMT passes, Kings Canyon National Park. At Franklin Meadow, a good spot for lunch, a major fork in the trail is reached. A substantial ascent eastwards up Evolution Valley leads to a rather problematic river crossing at Evolution Meadow. Then it is all plain sailing to McClure Meadow, which provides good camping areas near to Evolution Creek and marvellous views eastwards towards the high peaks of Mount Mendel (13,710ft), Mount Darwin (13,831ft) and Mount Spencer (12,431ft).

Return to the signboard above the **ranch** and turn right, signposted to Kings Canyon and the Piute Valley. The path climbs gradually, passing a large pond on the right, and after about 1.5 miles reaches a junction with the true line of the JMT, which was left yesterday to make the detour to Muir Trail Ranch. Those who did not have food caches at Muir Trail Ranch or did not need the campground there will have taken this more direct JMT route. You will know when you have reached this point as there is a signpost here which indicates Canada to the left and Mexico to the right, an inspiration to those superhuman backpackers who are attempting the whole route of the Pacific Crest Trail. Our route is a mere stroll compared to this ultra-marathon.

Turn right once more onto the JMT heading south-wards. In a short while pass on your right a surveyor's bench mark indicting a spot height of 7898ft (measured in the year 1947). Continue along the Trail, climbing very gradually up the valley amongst Jeffrey Pine and juniper trees. After 1.8 miles you reach Piute Creek. Cross this by a metal footbridge, so leaving the area designated as John

View from McClure Meadow looking up Evolution Valley

Muir Wilderness and Inyo National Forest and entering Kings Canyon National Park. The scenery becomes even more majestic as the path enters a rocky gorge. The roaring, tumbling, glissading waters of the South Fork of San Joaquin river are always at hand as the path climbs steadily into the heart of this mountain wilderness. After about 3 miles the JMT crosses the river by means of a sturdy metal footbridge and resumes on the opposite bank. The Trail continues for about another mile, fording a small creek and then the main river by means of a wooden plank bridge (ignore the path to the Goddard Pass on the west side of the bridge). This area, Franklin Meadow, is a good spot for lunch, and a good camping area for those who have gone far enough today.

On the far (east) side of the bridge the Trail heads to the left (north) for a couple of hundred yards before beginning a steep zig-zagging climb up the Evolution Valley. Nearing the top of the steepest part of the climb, first the sound and then the sight of a series of cascades and water slides are encountered. The climb eventually levels as the upper valley is reached. Continue ahead, climbing eastwards up Evolution Valley on the joint JMT/PCT.

It is necessary to ford the river to attain the path on the northern side of the valley. There are two recommended crossing points; the lower one is said to be more difficult when the river is high. In dry conditions the water level will possibly be less than 1ft. This is one river crossing, however, on the JMT that can be particularly problematical at times. If there is need for concern then be sure to ask Rangers and approaching walkers who should give good and useful information on river conditions and advice on tackling the crossing. At Evolution Meadow the path on the northern bank of the river climbs gradually to reach the verdant **McClure Meadow** with its magnificent panorama of the cirque of mountains to the east. There is a good **campsite** about 100yds after the ranger's hut (the latter is easily missed when walking east) – it is on a short side-trail to the left.

DAY 13

*McClure Meadow via Muir Pass
to Unnamed Lake North-East of Helen Lake*

Total distance of stage:	12.2 miles
Cumulative distance from Yosemite:	144.4 miles
Total ascent for stage:	2450ft
Total descent for stage:	1300ft
Cumulative ascent from Yosemite:	27,850ft
Cumulative descent from Yosemite:	20,850ft

Today's stage crosses the JMT's most famous pass, named after the great man himself. Muir Pass at 11,955ft misses the magical 12,000ft contour by less than 50ft, but nevertheless is the highest point by far reached on the Trail to date. It signals your entry into the really high country of the south. It also has the distinction of being the only pass on the JMT on which stands a man-made construction, a

Location	Height (ft)	Distance (miles)	
		Sectional	Cumulative
McClure Meadow	9650	0	0
Evolution Lake	10,880	3.3	3.3
Sapphire Lake	10,950	2.1	5.4
Northern end of Wanda Lake	11,480	2.0	7.4
Muir Pass	11,955	2.3	9.7
Helen Lake	11,620	0.6	10.3
Unnamed lake north-east of Helen Lake	10,800	1.9	12.2

Maps: Harrison Map Sheets 6 and 5

small stone shelter, the Muir Hut, built by the Sierra Club in 1930 for emergency use. En route to the pass the Trail climbs a series of mountain shelves on which are situated beautiful lakes whose crystal-clear waters reflect the surrounding high peaks. The route increases in both altitude and grandeur, passing first Evolution Lake and then Sapphire Lake. The high peaks hereabouts are named after life scientists such as Mendel and Darwin who worked on theories of genetics and evolution. The fragile and constantly changing nature of the mountain landscape as it is eroded and sculpted was clearly demonstrated to the author when he witnessed from Sapphire Lake a gigantic rockfall from the side of Mount Spencer. A barren, daunting, majestic world greets the walker in the upper sections of the ascent as the Trail follows the north-eastern shore of the massive Wanda Lake, touches the higher Lake McDermand and climbs to the summit of the Muir Pass.

Southern and eastern views are no less spectacular as the walker descends to Helen Lake, just below and east of the pass. The height means that there is no vegetation, only stony and barren ground that does not provide comfortable camping. Better to descend further to another, unnamed, lake to the east where good places on grass can be found for pitching the tent. And what a place to spend the night! True lovers of the high mountains will have found their spiritual home.

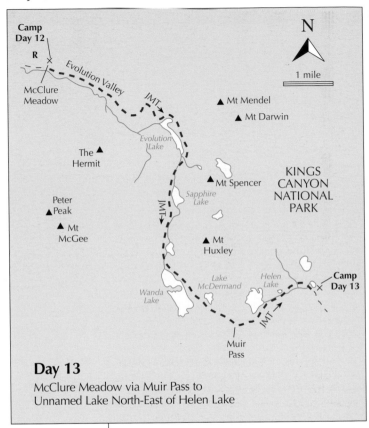

**Camp
Day 12**

R

Evolution Valley

McClure
Meadow

JMT

N

1 mile

▲ Mt Mendel

▲ Mt Darwin

Evolution
Lake

The ▲
Hermit

▲ Mt Spencer

**KINGS
CANYON
NATIONAL
PARK**

Peter
▲ Peak

Sapphire
Lake

JMT

▲ Mt
McGee

▲ Mt
Huxley

Lake
McDermand

Helen
Lake

**Camp
Day 13**

Wanda
Lake

JMT

Muir
Pass

Day 13

McClure Meadow via Muir Pass to
Unnamed Lake North-East of Helen Lake

A gentle introduction to the day. Leave the **camping
area** and continue on the Trail up the valley, passing
Colby Meadow. A couple of miles or so from McClure
Meadow reach a river crossing where multiple branches
of the river must be crossed. This is not too difficult in
dry conditions, but a crossing could be problematic
when the river is high. Soon after this river crossing
the route begins a long climb of about 1000ft into the
upper **Evolution Valley**. The scenery becomes wilder

Evolution Lake

and grander with each step. The next 1.5 miles or so provides easy waking among spectacular high alpine scenery as the Trail skirts to the east of the convoluted **Evolution Lake**.

At its southern end the JMT crosses the inlet stream of the lake by means of a long series of good stepping stones. The Trail climbs a little to pass to the west of **Sapphire Lake** and then climbs the next shelf to cross the lower ridge of the towering Mount Huxley to reach another (unnamed) lake. High mountains and snow-fields abound in this fabulous area. Another slight rise brings the hiker to the mile-long **Wanda Lake**. Those who wish to stop for the night prior to crossing Muir Pass are warned that there are no camping spots anywhere after this lake, until well over the pass. The Trail follows the north-eastern shore of this lake, climbing slightly to pass to the west of **Lake McDermand** before making the final ascent to the top of **Muir Pass** (11,955ft), where there is a stone shelter for emergency use. The views in

The JMT below Muir Pass

all directions of high mountain peaks, ridges and tarns are absolutely tremendous. The scene is typically high alpine, of stark, austere, barren, rocky beauty.

Descend eastwards from the pass. The path descends about 300ft to the southern end of **Helen Lake**. The Trail passes the south-eastern end of this lake over undulating ground before dropping to a small mountain tarn. Cross the inlet stream followed by the outlet stream of this high unnamed lake before plunging down a gully and on down the mountainside on a brilliantly engineered path to reach a second, somewhat larger lake on the edge of the treeline. This is a really super location in which to make **camp**. Do note, however, that there are relatively few pitches available, and if other hikers are already camped here for the night, it may be necessary to continue for about a mile further (and 1000ft lower) where further pitches may be found.

DAY 14

*Unnamed Lake North-East
of Helen Lake to Deer Meadow*

Total distance of stage:	11.3 miles
Cumulative distance from Yosemite:	155.7 miles
Total ascent for stage:	1000ft
Total descent for stage:	2900ft
Cumulative ascent from Yosemite:	28,850ft
Cumulative descent from Yosemite:	23,750ft

Location	Height (ft)	Sectional	Cumulative
Unnamed lake north-east of Helen Lake	10,800	0	0
Big Pete Meadow	9150	2.8	2.8
Little Pete Meadow	8850	0.9	3.7
Le Conte Canyon	8780	0.7	4.4
Kings river/Mather Pass Trail Junction	8070	3.4	7.8
Deer Meadow	8880	3.5	11.3

Map: Harrison Map Sheet 5

After the rigours of the long, arduous climb to the Muir Pass yesterday, and the steep descent to the treeline afterwards, today offers a relatively easy day, valley walking through lush high alpine meadows and magnificent forests. It offers time to recover from the high mountains for a brief while and to prepare for the onslaught of a succession of high passes during the next few days. For those, hopefully, small numbers of hikers who, for whatever reason, must leave the Trail there is an excellent trail eastwards over Bishop Pass and on to the small town of Bishop where all facilities are found. But even this escape route will take at least a couple of days of hard

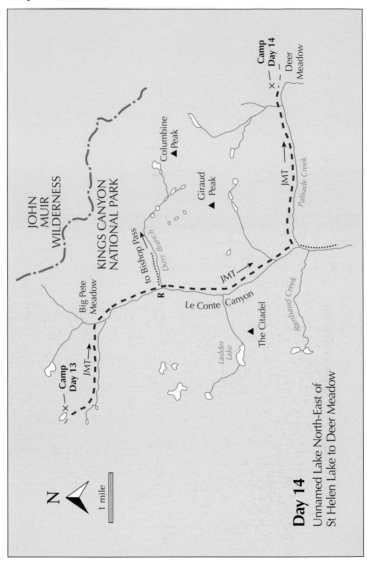

N

1 mile

Day 14
Unnamed Lake North-East of
St Helen Lake to Deer Meadow

effort. You are deep inside one of the most spectacular wildernesses in North America.

A long, gentle descent southwards down Le Conte Canyon leads to a major trail junction. The JMT turns to the east here to follow Palisade Creek. After several miles of gradual ascent up this valley Deer Meadow is reached at the foot of the famed 'Golden Staircase'. Deer Meadow offers good camping. Tomorrow is to be a big day, so be sure to have plenty of both rest and food.

From the unnamed lake where you spent the night the path descends steeply, soon crossing and then following the course of the river. The scenery down the valley is of high quality with sheer rock faces dominating. Care is required with your footing on this descent. On the journey a couple of high meadows are passed, **Big Pete Meadow** and Little Pete Meadow, but nobody seems to know who these characters were. After about 4.5 miles reach a ranger station which is hidden about 50yds to the right of the path, among lakes. This is Le Conte Canyon.

In Le Conte Canyon

At this point the Trail to **Bishop Pass** heads steeply up the valley to the left (east). For those who have lost their food, energy or time, and must retreat from the wilderness, this is the way to go. It will take about two days to reach South Lake Trailhead by this route (South Lake Trailhead is still another 22 miles from the town of Bishop, and this being the US there is no public bus service from the trailhead to Bishop).

The JMT does not take this escape route, but rather continues on down the valley to the south on an easy path that leads in 3.3 miles to a trail junction. Bear left at this point to ascend the valley to the east, following the signpost to the Mather Pass (11.5 miles). The lower end of the valley has a fairly gentle gradient, and the first few miles up to **Deer Meadow** are on a gradually rising path through the trees. There are several **camping** areas among the trees in Deer Meadow. Note that if you make the decision not to camp here then there is no other suitable place until you reach the Palisade Lakes 1700ft above you. An overnight stop here is therefore highly recommended. Note that in 2002 a forest fire burned trees in Deer Meadow and the trail was re-routed to the left. There are, however, still several sites available for camping.

DAY 15

Deer Meadow via Mather Pass to Kings River

Total distance of stage:	12.0 miles
Cumulative distance from Yosemite:	167.7 miles
Total ascent for stage:	3300ft
Total descent for stage:	2000ft
Cumulative ascent from Yosemite:	32,150ft
Cumulative descent from Yosemite:	25,750ft

One of the really great days on the JMT. The zig-zagging path of the Golden Staircase is a marvel of mountain engineering and leads up, not exactly effortlessly, to a high

Location	Height (ft)	Distance (miles)	
		Sectional	Cumulative
Deer Meadow	8880	0	0
First Palisade Lake	10,620	2.8	2.8
Second Palisade Lake	10,720	1.0	3.8
Mather Pass	12,100	3.0	6.8
Upper Basin	11,200	1.3	8.1
Kings river camping area	10,160	3.9	12.0

Map: Harrison Map Sheet 4

JMT path in the Upper Palisade Valley

shelf in which sit the two Palisade Lakes. There is time for a long rest next to these pristine waters before continuing the ascent south-eastwards in the Upper Palisade Valley to the foot of the main climb to the Mather Pass. Considerable effort will be required to reach the top of the Mather Pass (12,100ft), the first time the Trail has gone beyond the 12,000ft contour on this trip. The high

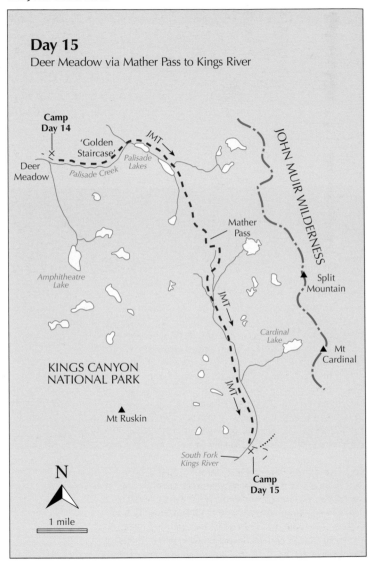

Day 15
Deer Meadow via Mather Pass to Kings River

Camp Day 14

Deer Meadow

'Golden Staircase'

Palisade Creek

Palisade Lakes

JMT

Mather Pass

Amphitheatre Lake

JMT

Cardinal Lake

JOHN MUIR WILDERNESS

Split Mountain

▲ Mt Cardinal

KINGS CANYON NATIONAL PARK

▲ Mt Ruskin

JMT

South Fork Kings River

Camp Day 15

N

1 mile

ridge to the east, on which lie the giants of Mount Bolton Brown (13,491ft), Mount Prater (13,471ft), Split Mountain (14,058ft) and Cardinal Mountain (13,396ft), forms the boundary of Kings Canyon National Park (east of this high crest lies the John Muir Wilderness area). A mountain desert landscape greets the walker on the southern side of the pass. A descent through this stark Upper Basin leads down to the trees and to the South Fork of the Kings river, where good campsites are found.

Try to make an early start today, as then you should be able to climb up the Golden Staircase (see below) in the cool of the early morning, before the sun hits its rocks.

From your campsite in **Deer Meadow** the trees are soon left behind as the climb begins on a superbly constructed path. One can only marvel at the tremendous feat of engineering required to build this path in such a remote area. After the first part of the climb you come to a long section of tight zig-zags known as the **Golden Staircase**. This leads to the upper valley (heaven?!),

Looking back at the Palisade Lakes during the ascent to Mather Pass

173

where the path takes you over to the right to look down onto Deer Meadow and the valley way below. Further climbing leads up to the first of the two **Palisade Lakes**. By now you will have accomplished half the total climb to the pass.

The path soon climbs above the northern shore of the lake to avoid the large rock slabs that plunge down to its waters and continues to traverse south-eastwards above both lakes. After the second lake the path rises and the pass comes into view. The terrain becomes more rocky and austere as the path zig-zags upwards. After what seems an age the path drops the last few feet to reach the **Mather Pass** (12,100ft). It will probably take you at least 4½hrs from Deer Meadow to the pass.

A desert landscape greets the eye to the south, with several small tarns dotting the dry, barren plain. A zig-zagging path drops the walker steeply down to the Upper Basin. Walk south down the basin. This easy angled terrain now makes for easy, fast walking. The path eventually reaches the treeline and descends to ford the Kings river. **Camping areas** can be found about 50–100yds after the river. Note that at this height (a little above 10,000ft) it is not permitted to light fires (national park regulations).

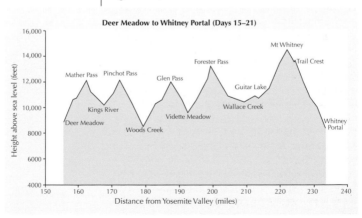

Deer Meadow to Whitney Portal (Days 15–21)

DAY 16

Kings River via Pinchot Pass to Woods Creek

Total distance of stage:	11.6 miles	
Cumulative distance from Yosemite:	179.3 miles	
Total ascent for stage:	2050ft	
Total descent for stage:	3700ft	
Cumulative ascent from Yosemite:	34,200ft	
Cumulative descent from Yosemite:	29,450ft	

Location	Height (ft)	Distance (miles)	
		Sectional	Cumulative
Kings river camping area	10,160	0	0
Lake Marjorie	11,110	2.8	2.8
Pinchot Pass	12,130	1.8	4.6
JMT/Sawmill Pass Trail Junction	10,340	3.6	8.2
JMT/Paradise Valley Trail Junction	8520	3.3	11.5
Woods Creek Suspension Bridge & camping area	8500	0.1	11.6

Maps: Harrison Map Sheets 4 and 3

Another pass of over 12,000ft is tackled today, but the ascent of Pinchot Pass (12,130ft) is a fairly minor affair compared with yesterday's epic, and the two monsters, Glen and Forester passes, are yet to come. There is more sublime country as the trail passes several lakes on its ascent, the most notable and largest being Lake Majorie. Pinchot Pass is the col between Mount Wynne (13,179ft) to the east and Crater Mountain (12,874ft) to the south-west. Mount Pinchot itself lies to the north-north-east of the pass.

A very long descent follows from Pinchot Pass, leading to the west of the twin lakes, from where Woods Creek is followed for many miles to a major trail junction. Here is found the most impressive suspension

Day 16

Kings River via Pinchot Pass to Woods Creek

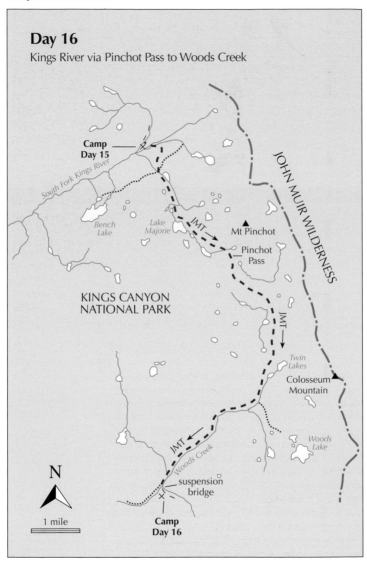

The JMT path between the Kings river and the Pinchot Pass

bridge on the whole of the JMT, over the creek to Woods Creek campsite, a popular spot with hikers at the junction of the JMT and a trail westwards out to the Cedar Grove roadhead.

Leave the **campsite** and almost immediately begin a gradual climb. Cross a river and ascend through the trees. Before leaving the wood you will come to a trail junction to Taboose Pass on the left. Ignore this, cross another river and leave the trees to enter an upper meadow. Ignore the trail on the right to Bench Lake and continue ahead passing an unnamed tarn over to the left. The Trail is fairly level for a while. Cross a couple of streams to approach **Lake Marjorie**. The JMT then winds its way uphill towards the col. Soon the zig-zags begin which will lead the walker easily(!) to the top of the pass. **Pinchot Pass**, at 12,130ft, is a mere 30ft higher than the previous pass, Mather Pass. However Pinchot Pass is the easiest of the high cols of the southern JMT to reach, as the valley to the north lies at about 10,000ft.

Mountain landscape south of the Pinchot Pass

Yet another truly magnificent alpine scene greets the walker on his or her arrival at this pass.

Descend southwards steeply down the zig-zags to reach an upper basin from where the path descends more gradually. This path heads south-west down the valley for about 7 miles to reach a trail junction. Here there is a signboard indicating the JMT, Rae Lakes Ranger Station and the Glen Pass (8.9 miles to Glen Pass). All these destinations lie straight ahead. To the right is a path signposted to Paradise Valley (5.5 miles) and Road's End(!) in 15.1 miles. Take the JMT path and within 100yds you will reach a most impressive suspension bridge over Wood's Creek. Cross this to enter the Wood's Creek **campground**, where two bear boxes (food storage boxes) should be found.

DAY 17

Woods Creek via Glen Pass to Vidette Meadow

Total distance of stage:	13.2 miles
Cumulative distance from Yosemite:	192.5 miles
Total ascent for stage:	3650ft
Total descent for stage:	2600ft
Cumulative ascent from Yosemite:	37,850ft
Cumulative descent from Yosemite:	32,050ft

Location	Height (ft)	Distance (miles)	
		Sectional	Cumulative
Woods Creek suspension bridge & camping area	8500	0	0
Dollar Lake	10,270	3.6	3.6
Rae Lakes	10,560	2.0	5.6
Glen Pass	11,978	2.6	8.2
JMT/Bullfrog Lake Trail Junction	10,650	3.1	11.3
Vidette Meadow	9560	1.9	13.2

Maps: Harrison Map Sheets 3 and 2

Another day, another pass. Glen Pass (11,978ft) is tanta-lisingly just below the magical 12,000ft contour line, but what it lacks in altitude it makes up for in the quality of the views from the top. A long approach walk up a beau-tiful valley passes first Dollar Lake and then Arrowhead Lake, all the time with the pointed fang of Fin Dome (11,693ft) towering above the valley to the west domi-nating the view. A natural causeway between the Lower and Upper Rae lakes leads the walker to the foot of the major ascent to the pass. The last section of the climb is over exceedingly steep ground, but as ever with the JMT, the gradient of the well-engineered path is not excessive.

Day 17

Woods Creek via Glen Pass to Vidette Meadow

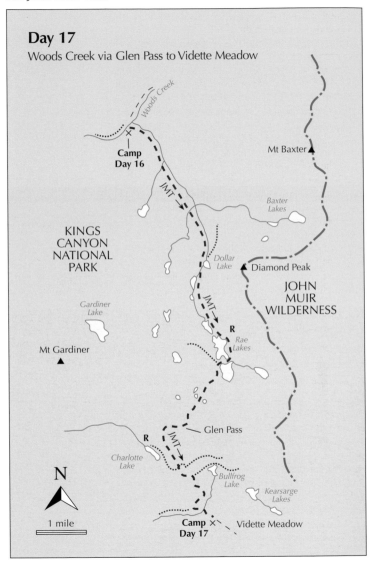

Woods Creek

✕ **Camp
Day 16**

JMT

Mt Baxter ▲

Baxter
Lakes

**KINGS
CANYON
NATIONAL
PARK**

*Dollar
Lake*

JMT

▲ Diamond Peak

**JOHN
MUIR
WILDERNESS**

*Gardiner
Lake*

R

*Rae
Lakes*

▲ Mt Gardiner

Glen Pass

R

JMT

*Charlotte
Lake*

*Bullfrog
Lake*

*Kearsarge
Lakes*

N

1 mile

✕ **Camp
Day 17**

Vidette Meadow

Yet another phenomenal view rewards the hiker for his or her efforts in reaching this point.

The descent southwards is initially very steep, but easier terrain leads down past several small lakes, with a view of the larger Charlotte Lake to the south-west. Several trail junctions, to Bullfrog Lake and to Kearsarge Pass, are passed on the way to a major junction near Bubbs Creek. To the right (west) lies a trail out of the wilderness to Roads End and Cedar Grove, but the John Muir Trail turns to the left (south-eastwards) to commence the long approach to the very last, and the highest, of the high passes on the JMT. But that is for the morrow. Vidette Meadows, a short distance from the last trail junction, provides a pleasant campground for the night, with superb views of the dramatic East Vidette (13,350ft) at the end of a long north–south mountain ridge

The Trail goes gradually uphill from the **campground** to reach **Dollar Lake** (camping not permitted) in just over 3.5 miles. Here there is a trail junction to Baxter Lake(s) to the left (east). Ignore this to continue along the JMT

Mountains above Rae Lakes

Fin Dome seen from the JMT above Woods Creek en route to Rae Lakes

up the valley, crossing a stream and then continuing above and to the left of another lake (Arrowhead Lake), all the while heading towards **Rae Lakes**. On reaching Lower Rae Lake note the perfect reflection of Fin Dome (11,693ft) in its waters. Continue to reach a path junction up to a ranger station. Ignore this and proceed ahead, passing another sign – this time to food storage boxes over to the right. The path takes the natural causeway between the Upper and Lower Lakes. Note that there is little chance of finding water (except for a detour to the two lakes on either side of Glen Pass) between the Upper Rae Lakes and Vidette Meadows at the end of the day. So be sure to stock up well with water at Rae Lakes.

On the far side of the causeway the steep climb up to Glen Pass begins. The climb can be considered in two phases. The first is an ascent to an upper stony plateau above a high tarn. A short level and descending section then leads to the base of the final steep climb up to the pass. From this plateau about half an hour of effort leads to **Glen Pass**, 11,978ft, a most incredible viewpoint. The views both forwards and back are truly wonderful. A long time will no doubt be spent here providing the weather conditions are favourable.

Take special care with your footing on the steep descent south from the top of the pass. The Trail passes a couple of mountain tarns. Eventually, after a short section of ascent, Charlotte Lake comes into view below. About 2 miles after the pass a trail junction is reached. Onion Valley and Kearsarge Lakes can be reached by a trail heading off to the left (east). Vidette Meadow, today's destination, is 2.4 miles from this point. About ¼ mile later reach a cross-paths. Again Onion Valley (7.5 miles) and Kearsarge Pass (3 miles) are to the left, and **Charlotte Lake** is 0.7 miles to the right. The JMT sign-posted to Cedar Grove (1.8 miles) lies straight ahead. Yet another junction will appear quite soon. Here to the left is a trail to **Bullfrog Lake** (0.5 mile) and **Kearsarge Lakes** (3 miles). Once again proceed ahead on the JMT south, signposted to Vidette Meadow (1.2 miles). A steep zig-zagging descent soon follows which leads to yet another

Looking down from the top of Glen Pass (the path of the JMT is clearly visible on the right of the lake)

track junction. Right is a trail for Cedar Grove, but for the JMT and Forester Pass (7 miles) turn left. **Vidette Meadow camping area** is found about ½ mile from this junction. This campground should also have bear boxes for food storage (as bears can be a problem in this area, you are advised to store food in the bear boxes, but camp well away from them).

The shapely cone of East Vidette (13,350ft) towers above the campsite. It is especially attractive when bathed in evening or morning sunlight. It is daunting to speculate that tomorrow you will have to climb almost to the height of this peak in order to reach the top of the Forester Pass (13,180ft)!

DAY 18

Vidette Meadow via Forester Pass to Tyndall Creek

Total distance of stage:	12.0 miles	
Cumulative distance from Yosemite:	204.5 miles	
Total ascent for stage:	3800ft	
Total descent for stage:	2500ft	
Cumulative ascent from Yosemite:	41,650ft	
Cumulative descent from Yosemite:	34,550ft	

Location	Height (ft)	Distance (miles)	
		Sectional	**Cumulative**
Vidette Meadow	9560	0	0
JMT/Center Basin Trail Junction	10,500	2.4	2.4
Unnamed tarn below Junction Peak	12,240	3.5	5.9
Forester Pass	13,180	0.9	6.8
JMT/Lake South America Trail Junction	11,200	4.4	11.2
JMT/Shepherd Pass Trail Junction	10,900	0.6	11.8
Tyndall Creek camping area (Frog Ponds)	10,850	0.2	12.0

Maps: Harrison Map Sheets 2 and 1

Forester Pass, the main objective for today's hike, marks the boundary between two national parks, Kings Canyon and Sequoia. With the exception of Trail Crest on the side of the Mount Whitney massif (which is not technically on the JMT, and certainly is miles from the PCT), Forester Pass at 13,180ft is the highest point reached on both the John Muir Trail and the whole of the Pacific Crest Trail. Junction Peak (13,888ft) to the east of the pass is one of the most impressive mountains in this region of the Sierras, a massive tower of rock that dominates the scene on the climb to the Forester Pass.

Not only is Forester the highest pass on the JMT, but many consider it to be the finest. The final approach to the

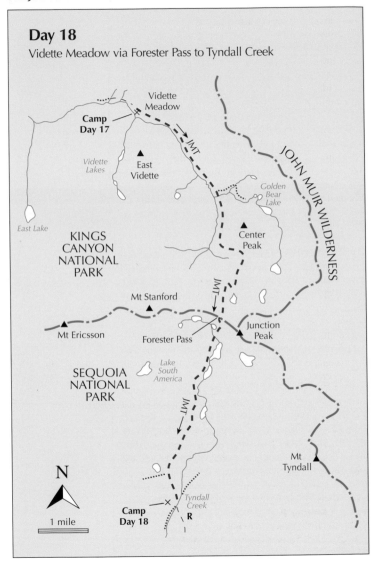

Day 18

Vidette Meadow via Forester Pass to Tyndall Creek

pass is in outstanding mountain country – rocky, stark and impressive. The view from the summit of the surrounding high peaks is second to none in a landscape that is full of superlatives. The pass is the easiest cut in the Kings Kern Divide a long, high ridge which runs from Junction Peak westwards to Mount Stanford (13,973ft), Mount Ericsson (13,608ft), Mount Geneva (13,059ft), Mount Jordan (13,344ft) and Thunder Mountain (13,588ft).

Perhaps the most sensational section of the whole engineered John Muir Trail is the initial descent southwards from the Forester Pass, but later the drop down into the valley is more gradual. By taking this trail you leave Kings Canyon National Park and enter Sequoia National Park. The day ends with a short ascent to reach Tyndall Creek, where lovely views will be enjoyed on your night's stay here.

The path from **Vidette Meadow** rises gradually for the first few miles, passing after about 2.5 miles, an unmarked trail junction for Center Basin, which is off to the left. This junction is situated at an altitude of 10,500ft. Ignore this junction, but instead continue up the valley soon passing an obvious camping area with a bear box to the right of the path, by the river, approximately 30ft below the path level. There may also be a note here indicating that hanging food is useless in this area: the bears will get it anyway!

The Trail passes some camping areas to the right of the path before bearing to the left to cross a relatively flat area where a small, unnamed lake is situated. The landscape becomes more rocky and austere. The JMT slowly climbs to reach a small mountain tarn beneath the towering rocky summit of **Junction Peak** (13,888ft). Words will probably fail those who attempt to describe this magnificent natural amphitheatre. The switchbacks take the hiker slowly but surely up to the col, around 950ft above the tarn. **Forester Pass** will be your first experience of being above 13,000ft on this trip. In the author's opinion this is the most sensational perch of the many on the John Muir Trail.

The JMT heading upwards towards the Forester Pass

The first part of the descent is an almost unbeliev- able route down a superbly engineered path, first by tight zig-zags on the west side of the gully, then crossing over the latter to descend the huge rock face on an excellent path. At the bottom of the rock face pick up the path which heads south across and gradually down the mas- sive desert-like upper basin. Be sure to look back several times to be amazed at the incredibly steep gully and rock face that you have just descended. Pass through an area of trees, emerging once more into the open. Immediately before entering trees for a second time you will meet a trail junction: to the right is the path to **Lake South America** (3.1 miles) and the Kern river (3.2 miles). Ignore this and remain on the JMT, heading down into the trees. Soon the Trail bears left to cross a creek, and a few yards later reach another track junction: left lies the path to Shepherd Pass (3.4 miles). Ahead is your trail signposted to Wallace Creek (4.4 miles, and to Mount Whitney, 16.1 miles). This is the first real indication that the end of the trail is in reach: the highest mountain in continental US marks the end of the JMT!

Junction Peak, which lies to the east of Forester Pass

The descending trail from the top of Forester Pass

Continue ahead downhill. A few minutes later you should reach a signpost and path off to the right to a ranger station. Ignore this and walk straight ahead on the JMT. The path climbs through woodland for about 10–15mins to reach a food storage container (bear box) and the **Tyndall Creek camping area (Frog Ponds)**. Note that no fires are allowed here (at about 11,000ft, this is prohibited by the park authorities). There are lovely reed-filled tarns just a few yards from this campsite, situated in a gorgeous location where the evening sunlight on the surrounding mountains can be enjoyed.

DAY 19

Tyndall Creek to Guitar Lake

Total distance of stage:	12.1 miles
Cumulative distance from Yosemite:	216.6 miles
Total ascent for stage:	1800ft
Total descent for stage:	1200ft
Cumulative ascent from Yosemite:	43,450ft
Cumulative descent from Yosemite:	35,750ft

Location	Height (ft)	Distance (miles)	
		Sectional	Cumulative
Tyndall Creek camping area (Frog Ponds)	10,850	0	0
Wallace Creek	10,400	4.8	4.8
JMT/PCT Rock Creek Trail Junction	10,860	3.2	8.0
Crabtree Ranger Station	10,680	1.1	9.1
Timberline Lake	11,100	1.7	10.8
Guitar Lake	11,450	1.3	12.1

Map: Harrison Map Sheet 1

For the first time in several days there is no pass to be crossed today. In some respects today's walk is a fairly gentle prelude for the grand finale of Whitney that is to follow tomorrow. It traverses beautiful country and should be savoured to the full, as today marks the real end of your wilderness experience. Tomorrow, once the Whitney Ridge is attained, you will almost certainly not be alone!

The Trail first heads south with views westwards to the Kaweah Ridge above Kern Canyon. A few miles after crossing Wallace Creek the JMT turns eastwards to head for the high country of the Whitney massif. An optional visit to the ranger station at Crabtree is followed by an ascent, first passing Timberline Lake and finally reaching

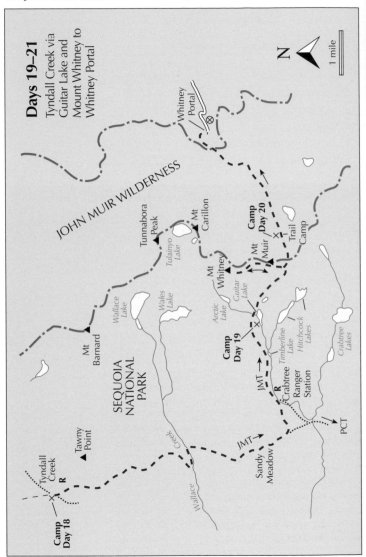

Days 19–21
Tyndall Creek via
Guitar Lake and
Mount Whitney to
Whitney Portal

N

1 mile

Whitney
Portal

JOHN MUIR WILDERNESS

Tunnabora
Peak

Mt
Carillon

Tulainyo
Lake

Camp
Day 20

Mt
Muir

Trail
Camp

Mt
Whitney

Guitar
Lake

Wallace
Lake

Wales
Lake

Arctic
Lake

Mt
Barnard

Timberline
Lake

Hitchcock
Lakes

Crabtree
Lakes

Camp
Day 19

JMT

Crabtree
Ranger
Station

R

PCT

SEQUOIA
NATIONAL
PARK

Tawny
Point

Sandy
Meadow

JMT

Wallace
Creek

Tyndall
Creek

R

Camp
Day 18

Guitar Lake, so named because of its interesting shape. From this, your overnight camp, Mount Whitney and the end of the JMT lie overhead to the east.

The JMT heads southwards from the **Tyndall Creek campsite**, heading for Wallace Creek. From the campsite the Trail climbs a little to reach and traverse a wide, high, desert-like plateau, with views over to the left towards the Mount Whitney massif and over to the right to the jagged Kaweah Ridge above Kern Canyon. The path then soon begins a gradual descent through woodland. After fording a stream the Trail descends more steeply, veering to the east to drop down to a trail junction at Wallace Creek. Here a path goes off to the right (west) to Junction Meadow (4.3 miles) and Kern Hot Springs (11.8 miles). Ignore this route but continue ahead on the JMT sign-posted to Crabtree Ranger Station (4.4 miles) and Mount Whitney (11.7 miles). Cross **Wallace Creek** by stepping stones and almost immediately pass to the left of a bear box (food storage) container (camping is possible here).

   Here begins an ascent of about 500ft, made easy by a series of zig-zags. The path levels and continues on an undulating route, passing **Sandy Meadow** and eventually dropping down to reach a trail junction: straight on leads to Lower Crabtree Meadow (0.7 miles) and Rock Creek (6.3 miles). However, this is not the way of the JMT, which bears left following the signpost for Crabtree Ranger Station (1.0 miles) and Mount Whitney (8.3 miles). This is an important place, for it is here that the mighty Pacific Crest Trail (PCT), which has been coincident with the JMT for much of the way since early on the hike, leaves its little sister trail to head off alone on its long continuing journey south to Mexico.

   The JMT path descends to a flat, sandy area. A pleasant walk through some beautiful pine trees, both living and dead, leads to a short rise and a trail junction and signpost. The path to the right leads in 0.2 miles to the **Crabtree Ranger Station**. This short diversion can be recommended; the ranger, billeted in this lonely but beautiful spot, will probably welcome your company for a short while, and there is a toilet and a water source nearby. To reach the ranger station descend and cross a stream to reach another trail junction and signpost, where there should also be a bear box (food storage) container. Right is to Lower Crabtree Meadow (1.1 miles) and Rock Creek (6.7 miles), but turn left for 0.1 mile to the ranger station.

Return to the JMT/ranger station path junction where you turn right to follow the Trail towards Guitar Lake. The path climbs gradually up towards the Whitney Ridge. **Timberline Lake** (camping not permitted) appears on the right at around the limit of the treeline, as might be expected from its name! Walk along the left (northern) edge of this reed-filled lake before climbing again up to the next rock shelf. Here is located **Guitar Lake**, so named because of its shape. Camping is not officially permitted on the grassy area next to the lake, although many campers do seem to use this area. Camping spots can be found a little way left of the path, up the hill slightly, and within 100yds or so of the inlet stream of Guitar Lake (or the outlet stream of the higher Arctic Lake). At around 11,400ft this will be the highest point at which you have camped so far on your journey across the High Sierras. Tomorrow night, if you stop at Trail Camp on the far side of Mount Whitney, you will spend the night at an even higher altitude.

A late afternoon dip in Guitar Lake is not for the faint-hearted, and will be sure to cool even the warmest of long-distance hikers!

There are severe problems concerning the disposal of human waste at Guitar Lake, caused by the very large number of people camping there (over 3000 in 2005). To quote from a Ranger's information sheet: 'Where did you bury your faeces?...One hiker's toilet is another backpacker's camp.' 'Wag Bags' (Toilet in a Bag) are now being provided near Crabtree Ranger Station (and at Whitney Portal) for use at Guitar Lake and east to Whitney Portal, including on Mount Whitney. There are suggestions that their use may become mandatory.

DAY 20

Guitar Lake via Mount Whitney and Trail Crest to Trail Camp; and the Ascent of Mount Whitney

Total distance of stage:	10.0 miles
Cumulative distance from Yosemite:	226.6 miles
Total ascent for stage:	3200ft
Total descent for stage:	2600ft
Cumulative ascent from Yosemite:	46,650ft
Cumulative descent from Yosemite:	38,350ft

Location	Height (ft)	Distance (miles)	
		Sectional	Cumulative
Guitar Lake	11,450	0	0
Trail Junction	13,500	3.3	3.3
Summit of Mount Whitney	14,496	2.1	5.4
Trail Junction	13,500	2.1	7.5
Trail Crest	13,600	0.2	7.7
Trail Camp	12,050	2.3	10.0

Map: Harrison Map Sheet 1

An ascent of Mount Whitney, the highest point in the 'Lower 48', is the goal of many Americans. Although very high (14,496ft), the climb to the peak by the normal route northwards from Trail Crest along the summit ridge holds no technical difficulties. The great majority who climb the mountain do so from Whitney Portal, many of them on a long day-hike. As a result they are often unacclimatised and so rather foolhardy. But the JMT hiker, who has spent the last three weeks gradually acclimatising during the long walk from the north, should have few or no altitude problems.

It is nevertheless a considerable climb from Guitar Lake up to the summit, but at least heavy backpacks can

NATIONAL PARK SERVICE
U.S. DEPARTMENT OF THE INTERIOR

MOUNT WHITNEY ELEVATION 14,496.811 FT.
JOHN MUIR TRAIL – HIGH SIERRA TRAIL
SEPTEMBER 5, 1930

THIS TABLET MARKS THE CONSTRUCTION OF THE HIGHEST TRAIL
IN THE UNITED STATES. BEGUN IN 1928. IT WAS COMPLETED IN 1930
UNDER THE DIRECTION OF THE NATIONAL PARK SERVICE WORKING WITH
THE UNITED STATES FOREST SERVICE.

Plaque on the summit of Mount Whitney

be left at Trail Junction at 13,500ft, with only a light load to be taken for the last 1000ft to the summit. Perhaps of all the days on the JMT this is the one that you will remember the most in the years to come – the day you reached the highest mountain in continental US. It hardly needs saying that the views from America's highest perch are truly outstanding.

The JMT technically terminates on the summit of Whitney, but no one seems to know why! Unless you intend to spend the rest of your days up there, which incidentally would break Sequoia National Park regulations (!), you have to descend down to civilisation. The rest of the world can be accessed from Whitney Portal, the roadhead to the east of Mount Whitney, so this is the way to go. One more col has to be crossed and this, Trail Crest (13,600ft), is the highest pass on the whole journey. A seemingly never-ending trail leads down to Trail Camp, which if you stay here will break another Trail record: it is the highest campsite on the whole trek at about 12,000ft.

An early start is recommended so that all or most of the climb to the trail junction to Mount Whitney can be achieved in shade. Mount Whitney presents a huge and elongated mass of rock looming to the east of Guitar Lake, and as such blocks out the sun for several hours after dawn.

Leave Guitar Lake camping area to climb a little before descending slightly to a smaller, upper tarn (the last water until Trail Camp after climbing Mount Whitney). Resume the ascent, soon reaching the start of the many wide switchbacks that make the ascent of this very steep hillside a relatively easy affair (although you may not agree at the time!). Perseverance as always will lead you to a major trail junction at approximately 13,500ft. Do not confuse this with Trail Crest, the last and highest col on the hike. This will come later in the day (there is still a tiny bit more climbing to do even after you have reached the summit of Whitney!). This is the major junction, sometimes known as Trail Junction, where the path to Trail Crest and Whitney Portal meets the JMT. The path to the left leads to the summit of Mount Whitney in 1.9 miles. Whitney Portal is signposted as 8.7 miles from this junction. It cannot be over-stressed that the ascent of Mount Whitney should not be attempted if there are dark clouds building, particularly after midday; lightning strikes are common in such circumstances and are often fatal.

Alas, at this point the wilderness experience that you have enjoyed since leaving Yosemite will probably be over! You will no doubt meet hordes of walkers now coming up the trail from Whitney Portal to climb the highest mountain in continental US (Mount McKinley in Alaska is considerably higher). But on the positive side you will realise that it is not necessary to haul your heavy backpacks, which have been your constant burden since the start of this adventure, to the very top of the mountain. Backpacks can be left here, but do be sure to take adequate quantities of warm clothing, food and drink with you, and as there are quite a few people wandering around this area it isn't to be recommended to

It is important to take adequate quantities of water with you from the Guitar Lake camping area, as soon after leaving camp you pass the only water source between here and Trail Camp on the other side of Mount Whitney – day's end, a distance of about 9 miles and several thousand feet of ascent and descent. Only you can decide what is an 'adequate' amount of water to carry, but remember that you are going to a very high altitude where it is extremely important to drink plenty of water, and there will be no opportunity at all today to take shelter under trees from the fierce sun, as the Trail remains above the treeline at all times.

Rock spire passed en route to Mount Whitney summit

leave valuables here either. Another word of warning: do not leave any food in your backpacks as, although there is no risk of bears at this altitude, there are marmots and other rodents about that may chew into your pack to obtain food (fortunately you should not by now have large quantities of spare food). It goes without saying that a camera is an absolute must. This will be the first walking without a backpack since the ascent of Half Dome, which will no doubt seem like half a lifetime ago. Absolute purists, and those who trust neither man nor animal, will probably want to carry their backpacks up to the top of America. It is a round trip from here to the summit of Mount Whitney and back of around 4 miles, with about 1000ft of ascent and descent, but remember that at this altitude a mere 1000ft will seem much harder than an equivalent altitude gain at lower levels.

Even without a backpack the effects of the high altitude will almost certainly be felt. The path climbs the rocky ridge, weaving in and out on a narrow wandering path between shattered pinnacles and crests, to pass below and to the west of the rather minor summit named after John Muir himself (**Mount Muir**, 14,015ft). Care is required, particularly in windy weather. The route passes above three or four dramatically steep gullies on its way towards the summit. The hut on the top of the summit can be seen a very considerable time before it is reached! The ridge broadens and the trail crosses a giant scree and boulder field. In a few places it is rather indistinct, but it should be well cairned. The final concave slope eventually relents and the summit hut is then soon reached. The actual top of **Mount Whitney**, and continental US, is a short distance from the hut and no doubt will have quite a gathering of people around it. The plaque at this point declares a height above mean sea level of 14,496.811ft. You will probably want to spend a fair amount of time up here on the roof of North America enjoying the fabulous long distant view, celebrating the ascent of this high mountain and your completion of the JMT. Yes, the John Muir Trail officially finishes (or starts) here, but as public transport opportunities are extremely limited in the near

The hut on the summit of Mount Whitney

neighbourhood you will sooner or later need to descend back to Trail Junction and your waiting backpacks.

From Trail Junction leave the JMT for the last time to follow the path signposted to Whitney Portal, 8.7 miles, at first climbing very steeply for a few hundred yards to reach the col known as Trail Crest. This, at 13,600ft, is the highest point reached on your whole journey between Yosemite and Whitney Portal, but not the highest point on the JMT, because it is not technically on that Trail. From here there is an extensive view to the east, looking way, way down to the wide Owens Valley, 10,000ft below. Your route lies in this direction.

Descend from Trail Crest, thereby leaving Sequoia National Park to re-enter the John Muir Wilderness and Inyo National Forest. The pointed rocky peak of Mount Muir, which was by-passed on the route to Whitney, is seen to good effect on the first stages of this long descent. From Trail Crest the path drops around 2000ft in many zig-zags down to the mountain tarn at **Trail Camp**. This is a popular site beneath towering Mount Whitney, and at 12,000ft or thereabouts is the highest permitted camping area on the JMT. There is a solar toilet here.

Although rather a barren, rocky area that is often very overcrowded with campers, it is nevertheless a marvellous spot to spend your last night in the mountains on this epic journey. Extra care should be taken not to pollute the water here, and as always treat or filter water that you are to drink or use for food preparation.

Alternatively, if time is available and the bright lights of Lone Pine call strongly, there are two other campsites further down the valley, at Outpost Camp and at Lone Pine Lake. The latter can be recommended as it is situated in a very attractive setting and leaves a very short final day for the descent to Whitney Portal, and hopefully a lift to Lone Pine. But as most people will want to spend most of their time on Whitney and camp high for one last time, this stage ends at Trail Camp.

DAY 21

Trail Camp to Whitney Portal

Total distance of stage:	6.8 miles
Cumulative distance from Yosemite:	233.4 miles
Total ascent for stage:	50ft
Total descent for stage:	3700ft
Cumulative ascent from Yosemite:	46,700ft
Cumulative descent from Yosemite:	42,050ft

Location	Height (ft)	Distance (miles)	
		Sectional	Cumulative
Trail Camp	12,050	0	0
Mirror Lake	10,680	2.3	2.3
Lone Pine Lake	9,980	2.0	4.3
Whitney Portal	8,365	2.5	6.8

Map: Harrison Map Sheet 1

An easy walk down a mountain valley leads the long-distance hiker to Whitney Portal and journey's end. It is unlikely that you will be alone on this final walk, but few will be going in your direction. Most will be heading up the valley to the summit of Whitney. On reaching Whitney Portal all that remains is to hitch a ride down to Lone Pine and a long awaited and much needed hot shower – and food, glorious food!

From Trail Camp the Trail plunges steeply down the rocky valley to pass to the right of the aptly named Mirror Lake, with its reflections of the surrounding mountains (note that no wild camping is allowed here). Outpost Camp, a rather mosquito-infested area and not particularly recommended as a place to spend the night (it is often busy) is passed on the way down to Lone Pine Lake. The lake and camping area can both be reached on a short side-path off the main Trail.

Hikers on their last night on the JMT at Lone Pine Lake campsite

Continue on the Trail past Lone Pine Lake. Eventually you will reach the boundary of the John Muir Wilderness and Inyo National Forest. A few yards after this cross a

Dawn sunlight at Lone Pine Lake campsite

stream by stepping stones at North Fork Lone Pine Creek and continue downhill. After about a further 20mins the parking lot (car park) of Whitney Portal is reached at a tarmac road, the first since leaving Tuolumne Meadows, seemingly all those years ago. The altitude here is 8365ft, so you have descended over 6000ft since leaving the summit of Whitney. Turn right on the road to reach, within 50yds, the Whitney Portal General Store, the very heart of Whitney Portal! Indeed all Whitney Portal appears to be is this store and the large car park, used by inquisitive day-trippers and those attempting to climb Mount Whitney.

Souvenirs of your long hike can be purchased at Whitney Portal General Store, including cloth and metal badges and T-shirts of the JMT and of Mount Whitney, and of course postcards. But it will no doubt be the fast food on sale that will attract many Thru-Hikers. Hamburgers, sausages, cooked breakfasts and lunches are a speciality here, but a word of caution is perhaps not out of place: be careful how you indulge, as your stomach will not be used to such large and greasy quantities of stodge. The store is open 7 days a week during the summer hiking season from 7am until 9pm (last food orders at 7.45pm).

JMT hikers at Lone Pine Lake

There is a telephone at Whitney Portal store, but at the time of writing no international calls were available from it. So you will have to wait until you reach Lone Pine before informing loved ones at home that you have completed the Trail, climbed Mount Whitney and survived the bears. Whitney Portal also boasts a picnic area with toilets, and there is a water tap outside the general store (open daily from 8am to 8pm), where for the first time in more than a week it is not necessary to treat the water.

After a rest and food the next thought will be returning to civilisation. The first stage in this process is to get yourself to the town of Lone Pine, 13 miles down in the valley. This is by no means a straightforward task, as there is no public transport from Whitney Portal to Lone Pine. Unless you are a masochist and wish to walk all the way (don't even think about it!) a lift will have to be procured somehow or other. If you are a group of, say, more than three people then it will be best to split up into groups of two for this exercise. Try asking in the store to see if anyone is going down to Lone Pine and would be

Lone Pine

The town of Lone Pine is famous as the setting for several western and other American movies, but its main attraction these days is Mount Whitney. The demand for permits to climb Mount Whitney is incredibly high, and in order to keep down erosion on its over-used trails a strict permit quota/reservation system is in operation. Walkers holding a JMT wilderness permit automatically have access permission to the mountain.

Lone Pine is situated 13 miles downhill from Whitney Portal, beneath the eastern escarpment of the High Sierra, in the wide and low Owens Valley. In summertime the town and the valley experience very high temperatures. Highway 190 leads eastwards from Lone Pine to the notorious, sweltering Death Valley, lowest point in the western hemisphere (282ft below sea level), where the world's second hottest temperature was recorded (134°F in 1913). The lowest point in Death Valley is Badwater, which surprisingly is little more than 50 miles as the bird flies from the highest point in continental US, Mount Whitney, which towers nearly 15,000ft above Badwater. The high mountains on the east side of the Owens Valley, opposite Mount Whitney, are the White Mountains, home of the Bristle Cone Pine (*Pinus longaeva* and *Pinus aristata*), the most long-lived organism on the planet. Living specimens of the Bristle Cone Pine nearly 5000 years old have been found in the White Mountains. The Alabama Hills are a lower range of hills nearer to Lone Pine where many western movies have been filmed, including *How the West was Won*, *Hopalong Cassidy*, *Rawhide* and *Maverick*.

For help with accommodation and onward transport go to the Chamber of Commerce/Tourist Office in Lone Pine, which is located a few yards from the traffic lights (the only traffic lights!) in the town. Those seeking hostel accommodation should enquire from the owners of the cafe/store at Whitney Portal, who, in 2006, were having a hostel (dormitories and rooms) built in Lone Pine, close to Dow Villa. For a hot shower (if you are moving on without staying the night in a motel) try the hot showers at Kirk's Barbershop, 114N Main, Lone Pine. For leaving Lone Pine see 'Public transport to and from the trailhead' (in 'Planning Your Trip', above).

willing to give you a lift. As a last resort you can use the phone in the store to call a taxi up from Lone Pine. It may be inconvenient and not straightforward to get to Lone Pine, but compared to the 233 mile hike that you have completed it is surely a 'piece of cake'. Be patient and charming, and all will be well.

EPILOGUE

You will, I am sure, feel extremely proud of your achievement in conquering the JMT. But do try to keep things in proportion. A personal anecdote may illustrate how conceited one can become, and how easily deflated. A few weeks after returning home fresh from the success of hiking the JMT I spent a day on the Scottish hills with a friend. He brought another companion with him whom I had not met before. That evening in the pub I was waxing lyrical about the JMT and the ascent of Mount Whitney. 'It's over fourteen and a half thousand feet high you know', I boasted, before turning to my new acquaintance, who had been surprisingly quiet, to enquire as to the highest peak that he had climbed. He turned and half smiled: 'Everest', he said.

APPENDIX 1

Camping Areas on the JMT

The camping areas used on the JMT at the end of each day stage as described in this guidebook are listed below for reference. There are several other areas where it is possible to camp along the JMT, many of which are referred to at the relevant place in the text of the route.

One group of hikers gave their preference for camping at higher elevations than those suggested in this guidebook for the latter days on the Trail, from Tyndall Creek onwards. They found that higher camps were less prone to mosquitoes, offered wider views and provided quicker morning access to the next pass (at the expense of some ascent on the previous afternoon of course!).

Some of the camping areas listed below and recommended in this guidebook may be permanently or temporarily closed by the rangers at any time because of problems such as excessive erosion or environmental pollution, or because of bear activity in the area. In such cases do **not** camp there, but find a suitable alternative, hopefully not too much further along the JMT. Always 'look ahead' along the Trail, obtaining information from any rangers you may meet or from fellow hikers, particularly those coming from the direction in which you are heading.

The camping areas are listed from north to south along the JMT (from Yosemite to Whitney Portal):

- backpackers' campground at Yosemite Valley, before setting out on the trek

- a few yards off the JMT Trail, a little to the east of the Half Dome Junction (an alternative is the campground at Little Yosemite Valley)

- backpackers' camping area at Sunrise High Sierra Camp

- backpackers' campground at Tuolumne Meadows

- Upper Lyell Canyon (Lyell Bridge/Lyell Fork)

- campsite above the north shore of Thousand Island Lake

- backpackers' campground at the Devil's Postpile

- Deer Creek (the Reds Meadow Campground by the hot thermal baths would be an alternative, but a stay here would provide a very short day stage from the Devil's Postpile, and would necessitate a very long day afterwards to catch up on the itinerary, unless an extra day on the Trail is envisaged)

- Cascade Valley/JMT Trail Junction (the alternative is at Tully Hole, a mile before the Cascade Valley/JMT junction)

- Vermilion Valley Resort (a stay of two nights is recommended)

- Rosemarie Meadow

- backpackers' campsite near Muir Trail Ranch

- McClure Meadow

- on the eastern shore of the unnamed lake below and east of Helen Lake

- Deer Meadow

- Kings River

- Woods Creek

- Vidette Meadow

- Tyndall Creek

- Guitar Lake

- Trail Camp (a recommended alternative would be the lower Lone Pine Lake camping area).

APPENDIX 2

Ranger Stations along the JMT

Park rangers are stationed along the route of the JMT during the summer. Their responsibilities include upholding the regulations of the parks (for example, checking hikers for wilderness permits, and carrying out various conservation programmes including the building and repairing of hiking trails and combating the effects of path erosion). In addition they are also available to give advice to backpackers and assist if they are able in any emergency or accident. If you need to contact a ranger in the case of an emergency it is useful to be aware of the location of the various ranger stations along the route. These are listed below. Remember that not all the stations will be manned during the season and some may be closed in years to come. Remember also that rangers are often away working on projects in more remote parts of the parks for several days at a time, so may not be 'at home' at the time of your arrival.

Ranger stations from north (Yosemite) to south (Whitney) along the JMT are:

- Happy Isles (Day 1)
- Little Yosemite Valley (Day 1)
- Tuolumne Meadows (Day 3)
- Devil's Postpile (Day 6)
- McClure Meadow (Day 12)
- Le Conte Canyon (Day 14)
- Rae Lakes (Day 17)
- Charlotte Lake (Day 17)
- Tyndall Creek (Day 18)
- Crabtree Meadow (Day 19).

Note that the only form of man-made shelter available to hikers in the wilderness areas of the JMT is the Muir Hut on the top of the Muir Pass (Day 13). This is intended for emergency use only. Do **not** plan a stay here unless your health and/or survival depend upon it. There is also an emergency hut on the summit of Mount Whitney.

APPENDIX 3

Escape Routes on the JMT

Hopefully, all those attempting the John Muir Trail will experience good weather, easy river crossings and good health, and suffer no injuries or bear encounters (with resulting loss of food). However, hazards do exist, and it should never be forgotten that the Trail passes through vast areas of wilderness where, unlike on the Pennine Way or on a long route in the Alps, giving up is not simply a matter of continuing for another hour or two until a main road or village is reached. If your walk has to be curtailed, either permanently or temporarily, it is important to know the location of the nearest side-trails that lead out of the wilderness, and how long (usually at least half a day, often more) it will take to reach a road or settlement on foot.

Reaching a roadhead or even a village or small town in the United States is not usually the end of the problem. Public transport, particularly in the remote areas of the High Sierras, is often unavailable, and many backcountry roads are virtually unused by private cars. However, if you do encounter a car with passenger space in an area where people know there is a transport problem, you have a good chance of obtaining a lift. Remember that even in relatively large towns there may not be any public transport services.

The main side-trails of the JMT are listed below, from north (Yosemite) to south (Whitney). Some of these would also be of interest to those who wish to walk only a section of the JMT, as they could be used to join or leave the Trail at intermediate points along the way.

Note that the wilderness aspect of the Trail is more pronounced on the southern half of the JMT. There are several points at which relatively short and easy access/escape can be made until Muir Trail Ranch is left behind at the start of Day 12. From thereon until Whitney the JMT crosses very remote country, with relatively few escape routes, most of which involve the crossing of a high mountain pass on a trek of over a day's duration. Furthermore, although roads and resorts with food and other facilities are encountered on route or only slightly off-trail during the northern half of the Trail (Tuolumne Meadows, Reds Meadow, Vermilion Resort, Muir Trail Ranch) no such places are encountered on the southern half of the JMT after Muir Trail Ranch.

The term 'all facilities' below indicates restaurants, cafés, bars, grocery shops, motels and/or other accommodation, post office and ATM machine, but not necessarily a public transport connection. Mammoth Lakes, in the northern half of the Trail, and Bishop, in the southern half of the route, are the largest and best towns to head for if at all possible. They have all supplies and reasonable transport possibilities. The notes below on facilities along or near to the JMT refer only to the main summer season when the parks are open.

It should also be stated that although the author walked the JMT as described in this guidebook, he did not sample any of the escape route trails detailed below.

- **Day 1: Yosemite Valley**
  Harrison Map Sheet 13

  The northern terminus of the JMT. All facilities including restaurants and shops. Free shuttlebus to all areas of the Yosemite Valley complex. Bus to Merced.

- **Day 3: Tuolumne Meadows**
  Harrison Map Sheet 12

  Reached at the end of Day 3. Visitor Centre, food store and post office. Café which serves basic meals. Bus to Yosemite in the summer hiking season and road access to the town of Lee Vining (most facilities) to the east.

- **Day 5: Rush Creek Trail**
  Harrison Map Sheet 11

  Situated on the JMT between Donohue and Island passes. It is about 10 miles eastwards via Waugh Lake, Gem Lake and Agnew Lake to Silver Lake Resort (campground, ranger station). Road access to the small town of June Lake (most facilities). Allow at least a day.

- **Day 6: Shadow Lake Trail**
  Harrison Map Sheet 11

  Leave the JMT to follow the trail eastwards around the north side of Shadow Lake and then south-south-east past Olaine Lake to reach Agnew Meadows, about 3.7 miles from the JMT. Road access from here to the town of Mammoth Lakes (all facilities – particularly recommended for those who need to restock food supplies).

- **Day 6: Devil's Postpile**
  Harrison Map Sheet 10

  Reached at the end of Day 6. From here a shuttlebus runs during the summer hiking season to the Mammoth Mountain complex to the east, from where there is road access to the small town of Mammoth Lakes (all facilities).

- **Day 7: Reds Meadow Resort**
  Harrison Map Sheet 10

  En route during Day 7. Café which serves good basic meals. Food store. The resort is open only during the summer holiday season. Shuttlebus service during main summer season to Mammoth Mountain complex to the east, from where there is road access to the small town of Mammoth Lakes (all facilities).

- **Day 7: Mammoth Pass Trail**
  Harrison Map Sheet 10

  There are two trails that lead from the JMT – the first from Lower Crater Meadow (simply Crater Meadow on the Harrison Map) and a second from Upper Crater Meadow. Both lead in about 3.5 miles to the roadhead at Horseshoe Lake. From here there is road access to the small town of Mammoth Lakes (all facilities).

- **Day 8: Duck Lake Trail**
  Harrison Map Sheet 9

  It is just over 2 miles from the JMT/ Duck Lake Trail junction northwards up to Duck Pass (10,797ft). From here it is about a further 4 miles north-north-west to Coldwater Canyon Roadhead, where there is a campground and road access to the Mammoth Mountain complex and the town of Mammoth Lakes (all facilities).

- **Day 9: Edison Lake Trail (optional ferry) to Vermilion Resort**
  Harrison Map Sheet 8

  Vermilion Resort is reached at the end of Day 9. The resort is open only during the summer holiday season. Note that during periods of extreme drought, when the lake dries up considerably, both the ferry service and the resort may close. Vermilion Resort caters particularly for JMT and PCT hikers, and offers a wonderful service of accommodation, food, showers and hospitality. There is a store at the resort which stocks, along with normal food supplies, lightweight backpacking food and camping and backpacking equipment. The cooked meals on offer are first-rate in terms of both quality and quantity.

  Note that there is another resort further along the road from Vermilion, Mono Hot Springs Resort. This also offers food and accommodation, together with hot thermal baths.

- **Day 10: Bear Creek Trail**
  Harrison Map Sheet 8

  From the junction of the JMT with the Bear Creek Trail it is about 8 miles to a road that leads to Edison Lake. At the point where the trail meets the road it is a little over a mile to Mono Hot Springs Resort (see Day 9), and access to Vermilion Resort is also possible.

- **Day 11: Florence Lake Trail**
  Harrison Map Sheet 7

  Florence Lake is reached by a trail running nearly 5 miles westwards from Muir Trail Ranch. There is a ferry service across the lake during the summer season, or alternatively a roadhead can be reached along a trail running for a further 5 miles around the lake. The road leads both to Vermilion and Mono Hot Springs resort, but is a long way from any towns.

- **Day 12: Piute Creek Trail**
  Harrison Map Sheet 7

  Although this trail, which leaves the JMT at the point where the Trail enters Kings Canyon National Park, does offer a route out into the wider world it is a very long way out of the wilderness by this path. A route goes via Hutchinson Meadow and leads to a trailhead that eventually gives access to the town of Bishop (all facilities). At least two days and possibly three are required to reach the Pine Creek Trailhead, a distance of around 18 miles from the JMT junction.

- **Day 14: Bishop Pass Trail**
  Harrison Map Sheet 5

  The trail climbs steeply from Le Conte Canyon Ranger Station to the top of the Bishop Pass (11,970ft) in a little under 7 miles. It is a further 6 miles from there to South Lake Roadhead. From here it is around 22 miles by road to the small town of Bishop (all facilities).

- **Day 16: Taboose Pass Trail**
  Harrison Map Sheet 4

  A long and difficult escape route over the Taboose Pass (11,360ft), a distance of around 12 miles, to a roadhead over very steep terrain. The trail leaves the JMT by heading north-north-east from the vicinity of the Kings River. At least two days are required to reach the roadhead. This gives road access to the small town of Big Pine (most facilities).

- ### Day 16: Woods Creek Trail
  Harrison Map Sheet 3

  This trail junction with the JMT is reached at the end of Day 16. The trail heads westwards for around 20 miles to Cedar Grove roadhead, where there is lodging, a café and small store. Again, towns of any size are a long way off.

- ### Day 17: Kearsarge Pass Trail
  Harrison Map Sheet 3

  Two trails head eastwards from the John Muir Trail north of Bullfrog Lake to reach the top of Kearsarge Pass (11,820ft). A route continues eastwards via Flower, Gilbert and Pothole lakes to a roadhead in Onion Valley, a total distance of about 8 miles from the JMT. The road provides access to the small town of Independence (most facilities).

- ### Day 17: Bubbs Creek Trail
  Harrison Map Sheet 2

  This trail is encountered at day's end, a little before reaching Vidette Meadow camping area. It is a walk of about 14 miles westwards from the JMT at Vidette Meadow to Roads End Trailhead and Cedar Grove, where there is lodging, a café and small store. Towns of any size are still a long way away.

- ### Day 18: Shepherd Pass Trail
  Harrison Map Sheets 1 and 2

  A long and difficult two-day route leads north-east over Shepherd Pass (12,050ft) to reach Symmes Creek Roadhead in about 15 miles. This road gives eventual access to the small town of Independence (most facilities).

- ### Day 19: Pacific Crest Trail south via Rock Creek to Horseshoe Meadow
  Harrison Map Sheet 1

  The PCT leaves the JMT a little to the west of Crabtree Ranger Station. If the PCT is followed southwards for over 20 miles from the point at which it leaves the JMT it will lead, via Rock Creek and Cottonwood Pass (11,200ft), to a roadhead at Horseshoe Meadow. This road gives access to the town of Lone Pine (all facilities).

- ### Day 21: Whitney Portal
  Harrison Map Sheet 1

  The southern terminus of the JMT. The store here provides cooked food. The road leads downhill to the town of Lone Pine (all facilities).

APPENDIX 4

Bear Box Locations on the JMT

Below is a list of the location of bear boxes (food storage boxes) identified by the author in summer 2001 (it is possible that there are additional boxes in other locations). The locations of the boxes, of course, may change with time. Overall, the incidence of bear boxes is greater in the latter stages of the trek, between Woods Creek camping area and Crabtree Meadow (Days 16–19). The various national park and wilderness area authorities seem to have different policies with regard to bear boxes, and these may change in future. The number of bear boxes could therefore increase or decrease, or the boxes may even disappear altogether.

The best source of information for current bear box locations, that all trekkers are recommended to check out before travelling, is www.climber.org/scripts/BearBoxes.cgi?REG+ALL. This site lists all bear boxes in the Parks, not just those on the JMT.

The bear box locations below are listed from north to south along the JMT (from Yosemite to Whitney Portal).

- Yosemite Valley Campsite (Day 1 – Harrison Map Sheet 13)
- Sunrise High Sierra Camp (Day 2 – Harrison Map Sheet 13)
- Tuolumne Valley Campsite (Day 3 – Harrison Map Sheet 12)
- Devil's Postpile Campsite (Day 6 – Harrison Map Sheet 10)
- Reds Meadow Campsite (Day 7 – Harrison Map Sheet 10)
- Vermilion Resort (Days 9–10)
- Woods Creek camping area (Day 16 – Harrison Map Sheet 3)
- Rae Lakes camping area (Day 17 – Harrison Map Sheet 3)
- Vidette Meadow camping area (Day 17 – Harrison Map Sheet 2)
- Center Basin camping area (Day 18 – at junction of PCT and path to Center Basin – Harrison Map Sheet 2)
- Tyndall Creek camping area (Day 18 – Harrison Map Sheet 1)
- Wallace Creek (Day 19 – Harrison Map Sheet 1)
- Crabtree Ranger Station (Day 19 – Harrison Map Sheet 1)
- Lower Crabtree Meadow (Day 19 – Harrison Map Sheet 1)
- Lower Rock Creek Crossing (off route of Day 19 – on PCT)
- Rock Creek Lake (off route of Day 19 – on PCT)
- Lower Soldier Lake (off route of Day 19 – on PCT)

APPENDIX 5

Mountain Passes and Peaks on the JMT

The passes encountered on the John Muir Trail from north (Yosemite) to south (Whitney) are listed below.

Pass	Height (ft)	Day Stage	
Cathedral Pass	9700	Day 3:	Sunrise Camp to Tuolumne Meadows
Donohue Pass	11,056	Day 5:	Upper Lyell Canyon to Thousand Island Lake
Island Pass	10,203	Day 5:	Upper Lyell Canyon to Thousand Island Lake
Silver Pass	10,900	Day 9:	Tully Hole/Cascade Valley Junction to Edison Lake
Selden Pass	10,900	Day 11:	Rosemarie Meadow to Muir Trail Ranch
Muir Pass	11,955	Day 13:	McClure Meadow to unnamed lake north-east of Helen Lake
Mather Pass	12,100	Day 15:	Deer Meadow to Kings River
Pinchot Pass	12,130	Day 16:	Kings River to Woods Creek
Glen Pass	11,978	Day 17:	Woods Creek to Vidette Meadow
Forester Pass	13,180	Day 18:	Vidette Meadow to Tyndall Creek
Trail Crest	13,600	Day 20:	Guitar Lake to Trail Camp

Peak

Half Dome *(detour from the JMT)*	8836	Day 1:	Yosemite Valley to Half Dome Trail Junction/Sunrise Creek
Mount Whitney *(official end of JMT)*	14,496	Day 20:	Guitar Lake to Trail Camp

APPENDIX 6

Useful Addresses and Websites in the UK and US

John Muir Trust
Freepost, Musselburgh, EH21 7BR
tel: Membership Secretary 0845 458 8356,
email: membership@jmt.org
www.jmt.org

John Muir Birthplace Trust
126 High Street, Dunbar, East Lothian
www.jmbt.org.uk

The Map Shop
15 High Street, Upton-upon-Severn,
Worcestershire WR8 0HJ
www.themapshop.co.uk

Edward Stanford
12–14 Long Acre, London WC2E 9LP
or 39 Spring Gardens, Manchester M2 2BG
or 29 Corn Street, Bristol BS1 1HT
www.stanfords.co.uk

American Embassy
5 Upper Grosvenor Street, London W1
www.usembassy.org.uk

Travel Bureau (agents for Amtrak, US)
High Street, Wombourne, near
Wolverhampton WV5 9DN
Tel: 0800 6987545

Reds Meadow Resort
PO 395, Mammoth Lakes, CA 93546, US
www.redsmeadow.com

Vermilion Valley Resort
PO Box 258, Lakeshore, CA 93634, US
www.edisonlake.com

Muir Trail Ranch
Box 176, Lakeshore CA 93634 (spring and
summer address only)
www.muirtrailranch.com

Expedition Foods (specialist dehydrated
backpacking foods in the UK)
www.expeditionfoods.com

Adventure Foods (specialist dehydrated
backpacking foods in the US)
481 Banjo Lane, Whittier North Carolina
28789, US
www.adventurefoods.com

Bearikade – Wild Ideas (lightweight bear
barrels)
www.wild-ideas.net

**SIBBG (Sierra Inter-Agency Black Bear
Group)** (information on bears and details
of approved bear storage containers)
www.sierrawildbear.gov/foodstorage/
approvedcontainers.htm

Bearman's
www.yellowstone-bearman.com
The information on this website applies
specifically to Yellowstone bears and
grizzlies, but nevertheless provides good
general information on coping with bears,
precautions to take in bear country, the
actual (very low) level of risk, and how to
comport yourself in the presence of a bear.

The John Muir Trail

There are a huge number of websites devoted to John Muir, the John Muir Trail, the Californian Sierra Nevada, the relevant national parks and other related topics. A small sample of some of the more useful sites is given below, but the surfer will discover many more for him or herself.

John Muir

www.sierraclub.org/john_muir (a large website, called the John Muir Exhibit, on all aspects of John Muir's life)
www.djma.org.uk/jmbt (Dunbar John Muir Association)

Pacific Crest Trail Association

www.ptca.org

Pacific Crest Trail Association (JMT information)

www.pcta.org.jmt
www.pcta.org/about_trail/muir/over.asp

American National Parks Service

www.nps.gov

Sequoia and Kings Canyon National Parks

www.sequoia.national-park.com
www.nps.gov/seki

Yosemite National Park

www.nps.gov/yose
www.yosemitepark.com

Yosemite National Park Association

www.yosemite.org

Inyo National Forest (United States Forestry Service)

www.fs.fed.us/r5/inyo

Sierra Club of California

www.sierraclub.org

Amtrak Trains in the US

www.amtrak.com

APPENDIX 7

Bibliography

John Muir: The Eight Wilderness-Discovery Books

Diadem Books (1992)

John Muir: His Life and Letters and Other Writings

Baton Wicks Publications (1996)

John Muir Trail Country
by Lew and Ginny Clark.

A Western Trails Publication (1977)

On the Trail of John Muir
by Cherry Good.

Luath Press (2000). An excellent read of the places, life and times of John Muir. A comprehensive bibliography is included.

John Muir: from Scotland to the Sierra
by Frederick Turner.

Canongate Publishing (1997). A biography of John Muir.

John Muir's Wild America
by Harvey Arden.

National Geographic (1973), pp433–61

The John Muir Trail: Along the High, Wild Sierra
by Galen Rowell.

National Geographic (1989), pp467–92

John Muir, Nature's Visionary
by Gretel Ehrlich.

National Geographic (2000)

America's Wilderness: the photographs of Ansel Adams with the writings of John Muir
by Ansel Adams and John Muir.

Courage Books (1997). Outstanding photographs.

Guide to the John Muir Trail
by Thomas Winnett and Kathy Morey.

Wilderness Press (1978). The main American guidebook to the JMT. It describes the route in both directions.

Starr's Guide to the John Muir Trail and the High Sierra Region
by Walter A. Starr, Jr.

Sierra Club Books. This has been published for over 60 years and at the time of writing is into its 12th edition (1974). It includes a fold-out map. Several other trails connecting with the JMT are also described.

The Pacific Crest Trail: Southern California
by Jeffrey P. Schaffer, Ben Schifrin, Ruby Johnson Jenkins and Thomas Winnett

Wilderness Press (2003). This guidebook covers the section of the PCT from the Mexican border to Tuolumne Meadows, much of which, to Crabtree Meadows, follows the route of the JMT. The sister publication is *The Pacific Crest Trail: Northern California* by Jeffrey Schaffer (Wilderness Press, 2003), which covers the stages from Tuolumne Meadows to the Oregan border, none of which follow the JMT. Both guides contain colour topographical maps. These two guides replace the earlier single-volume Wilderness Press guidebook to the PCT in California, which had become something of a classic.

The Pacific Crest Trail Hiker's Handbook
by Ray Jardine

Adventure Lore (2nd edition, 1996; now out of print). Sound advice and useful tips from America's top backpacker. Much of what is written is also relevant to the JMT.

National Geographic's Guide to the National Parks of the United States
by Elizabeth Newhouse (2003).

Lots of useful data on the parks traversed by the JMT.

Bear Aware: Hiking and Camping in Bear Country
by Bill Schneider.

Falcon (2nd edition, 2001)

How to Shit in the Woods: an environmentally sound approach to a lost art
by Kathleen Meyer.

Ten Speed Press (2nd edition, 1994)

California

Lonely Planet (3rd edition). General travel guide to the state. Useful for general planning. Buy the most up-to-date edition.

US

Lonely Planet. General travel guide. Useful for general planning. Buy the most up-to-date edition.

Many publications by and about John Muir can be purchased from the John Muir Trust (see Appendix 6).

The Natural World

The High Sierra. The American Wilderness
by Ezra Bowen.

Time-Life Books (1980)

A Field Guide to California and Pacific Northwest Forests
by John Kricher and Gordon Morrison.

Peterson Field Guide Series. Houghton Mifflin Company (1998)

Sierra Nevada Wildflowers
by E. L. Horn.

Mountain Press Publishing Co. (1998)

Yosemite Wildflower Trails
by D. C. Morgenson.

Yosemite Natural History Association (1975)

California Mountain Wildflowers
by P. A. Munz.

University of California Press (1963)

The Audubon Society Field Guide to North American Wildflowers
by R. Spellenberg.

Alfred A. Knopf (1979)

The New Encyclopedia of Mammals
by David Macdonald.

Oxford University Press (2001)

Walker's Mammals of the World
by Ronald Nowak.

5th edn, vol. 1 (1991)

A Field Guide to Western Birds
by Roger Tory Peterson.

Peterson Field Guide Series. Houghton Mifflin Company (1961)

NOTES

LISTING OF CICERONE GUIDES

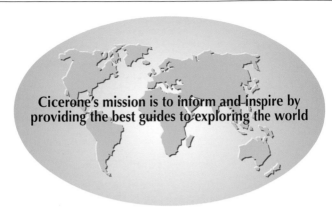

Cicerone's mission is to inform and inspire by providing the best guides to exploring the world

Since its foundation 40 years ago, Cicerone has specialised in publishing guidebooks and has built a reputation for quality and reliability. It now publishes nearly 300 guides to the major destinations for outdoor enthusiasts, including Europe, UK and the rest of the world.

Written by leading and committed specialists, Cicerone guides are recognised as the most authoritative. They are full of information, maps and illustrations so that the user can plan and complete a successful and safe trip or expedition – be it a long face climb, a walk over Lakeland fells, an alpine cycling tour, a Himalayan trek or a ramble in the countryside.

With a thorough introduction to assist planning, clear diagrams, maps and colour photographs to illustrate the terrain and route, and accurate and detailed text, Cicerone guides are designed for ease of use and access to the information.

If the facts on the ground change, or there is any aspect of a guide that you think we can improve, we are always delighted to hear from you.

Cicerone Press
2 Police Square Milnthorpe Cumbria LA7 7PY
Tel: 015395 62069 Fax: 015395 63417
info@cicerone.co.uk www.cicerone.co.uk

CICERONE